THE ROYAL DEAL

THE
ROYAL
DEAL

Making The Case for the One Everlasting Church

REV. PETER HENDRIKS OKELLO
3. R. DEAL TRILOGY

THE ROYAL DEAL:
Making The Case for the One Everlasting Church
Copyright © 2025 by Rev. Peter Hendriks Okello

Scripture taken from the HOLY BIBLE, NEW INTERNATIONAL VER-SION®. Copyright © 1973, 1978, 1984 International Bible Society. Used by per-mission of Zondervan. All rights reserved.

ISBN: 978-1-4866-2776-9

Cataloguing in Publication information can be obtained from Library and Ar-chives Canada.

Contents

INTRODUCTION

Please note that this book is written with the use of the New International Version (NIV). References to the triune God: Father, Son, Holy Spirit, begin with a capital letter, such as He, Him, His.

The THEME of this book: HOPE amidst HOPELESSNESS

In this book, entitled 'The Royal Deal,' we follow developments in today's life as part of and during this end-time period, leading up to the time of Jesus' return. As the KING of kings and the LORD of lords, Jesus' return will be accompanied by Christians who have honored and served Him as their Lord and Savior during their lives on this present earth. No one else than the Lord Jesus Christ, determines who will join Him in everlasting life on an everlasting, renewed earth that is most difficult to describe in terms of beauty, peace within a worldwide society difficult, if not impossible to imagine.

That everlasting reality is part of the final DEAL following the many developments and human struggles, as previous, today's and following generations will experience. We may remember that from the first book of the Bible, Genesis, we learn that our world, from the time Adam and Eve, the first two created persons, had already experienced the bad influence of Satan's power at work. That negative influence of Satan has had and continue to have its influence on past, present and following generations.

In the overall spectrum of present and future world events, the destructive influence of Satan on mankind, throughout the world, has been and continues to be a reality within all spheres of life. including Christian communities, such as families and churches. This fact of life is true and has been and still is noticeable in the destruction of many local churches and denominations in Western Europe during the 1970s-1990s. A similar destructive influence is presently occurring in North America as well, as it is expressed in the spiritual battle around the issue of immorality.

During the early years of 1900, a little more than hundred years ago, Dr. Abraham Kuyper, being a pastor before becoming a politician, gained the office of Prime Minister for four years, clearly understood the terrific danger of Pantheism within the context of Europe, as it rapidly approached the Netherlands (Holland). In efforts to stop this destructive power in overtaking Holland, Kuyper wanted the principle, called 'Sphere Sovereignty,' applied throughout the sphere of politics. I have elaborated on that matter in my book, *THE RIGHT DEAL: Making the Case for a More Respectful Society* (Amazon). This principle, among other things, guaranteed 'free speech' and the rights of fortitude for religious groups within a democratic society.

That freedom and right can (and will) only be applied and being effective within a so-called '*open*' secular society. That has been a situation enjoyed in Canada for a long time. Due to actions of our present Liberal government, we have noticeable descended into a '*radical*' secular society in which only one voice is allowed to be heard and taken seriously. The present, relevant question is 'how' to realize a possible return to that previous 'open' secular society. First, we need to pray for wisdom and God's interference and direction. After all, it is God who has the future in His hands, and who wants us to be involved in His work, direction and accomplishments.

Leaning on the Bible, this book is quite relevant in our times.

Next to speaking of political events in our own country and neighboring countries, we will look at the nation Israel, a special and peculiar country, located in the Middle East. This country was supposed to be non-existent following her destruction by the Roman Empire around AD 70. However, Israel was rather unexpectantly and officially 'reborn' in 1948, and will play a significant role during this end-time period, as we are already witnessing these days.

Chapters One to Three
Focus is on **Current End-time Developments.**

These end-time developments describe social and spiritual issues that are prevalent, though not related to each other, in today's societies.

Before turning to the subject of Israel in Chapter Two, we will gain some helpful insights in the development of the so-called Replacement Theology in Chapter One. This Chapter will discuss the wrong notion that the Church has replaced Israel following the events of AD 70. We will thereby take note of misgivings concerning the place and disappearance of Israel during the last 2000 years.

In Chapter Two, we will look intently at Israel's sufferings, whereby so many Israelites were forced to live in world-wide captivity. This overview of her world-wide sufferings will include her return to and restoration in the Middle East in 1948. We will hereby also hear about her place in present and future developments in her God-given place in the Middle East.

This attention for Israel developed through much personal study during the last number of years. It became apparent that the place of Israel in the world has been, and will remain, quite significantly, as she continues to receive repeated attention in world news. Thereby comes that no other 'people' have suffered so much as have the Jewish people. The approx. 60 million Jews killed during WW II is a significant sign of that terrible fact. Thereby comes a simmering but ongoing denial of their rightful, God-given place in the Middle East by many surrounding nations.

Born in the Netherlands at the beginning of WW II, I learned from my parents that we had a Jewish family as our neighbours before, during and following the war years of WWII. It was many years after the end of that horrible war in 1945, that I learned that my dad had helped our Jewish neighbors going underground and subsequently had to go underground himself. That knowledge, and having known our Jewish neighbours myself, has left me with a more than a little spot in my heart for Jewish people.

Chapter Three informs the reader about Satan's influence in leading many people, among them Christians, to accept sexual immoral lifestyles as norm. However, the Bible reminds people how wrong such a lifestyle is, and how to avoid and recover from it. APPENDIX A is helpful in reminding us why and how we need to avoid such lifestyles. Some examples of recovering from such lifestyles are provided.

Chapters Four to Nine

Focus is on **Anticipated End-Time Developments**.

The intent is that the related contents of those chapters may lead to a better understanding of what the Bible says about present and future developments in the world. The goal of these chapters is to understand what and how the various End-time developments will eventually lead to the time the Lord Jesus Christ will return, and together with His Church, will live eternally on a completely renewed earth. A *Royal Deal* indeed.

Please, join me in the following journey to gain a better understanding of the many present and future developments in the world, and especially in the Middle East. It is that part of the world that is not only prominent in the Bible, but also in present and future end-time periods, leading eventually towards the final return of our Lord Jesus Christ with His Bride, the one Church.

As reader you will notice that many Bible verses have been written out. One main reason for doing so is to accommodate readers of this book, by not having to look them up in their Bible. Another reason for writing out the many Bible texts is to enhance the notion that the Bible is the foundation of thinking and living as Christians in this tumultuous world and being in touch with the Lord Jesus Christ. It takes spiritual maturity to be able and willing to take a firm stand against strong and growing God-opposing forces in this present post-Christian era.

Remember that God's word is the one solid foundation that gives us, Christians, the ability to live God-pleasing lives. This is certainly true when we discern how to deal with serious, power-driven forces, when faced by worldly issues such as, for example, sexual immorality. Appendix A provides numerous O.T. and N.T. Bible passages to remind us how serious a problem such a lifestyle is. Remember, Satan, in his constant opposition to God and Jesus, read e.g. Matthew 4:1-11, uses this one important issue of immoral behavior to attack churches and Christian families in present and future God-opposing and denying world, a subject we will touch on in Chapter Three.

The first two Chapters are the result of my personal studies concerning the issue of Israel, as it has not been part of discussions and teachings in some churches, e.g. a denomination I am part of. It was only a number of years ago that I began to realize that, and how, Israel has been and still is playing an important role in our current end-time period.

Before you read this book, I would like to share with you the following words of wisdom written by Martin Luther to a friend of the Reformation:

> We cannot attain to the understanding of Scripture either by study or by the intellect. Your first duty is to begin by prayer. Entreat the Lord to grand you, of His great mercy, the true understanding of His Word. There is no other interpreter of the Word of God than the Author of this word, as He Himself has said,
>
> They shall be all taught of God.' Hope for nothing from your own labors, from your own understanding: trust solely in God, and in the influence of His Spirit. Believe this on the word of a man who has had experience. —*Ibid.*, b. 3, ch.7.[1]

The above words of advice from Luther to his friend, hundreds of years ago, are still valid in our time. Eventually, the Lord will return, and we all may long to experience that day being realized, as then our eternal lives will enter a marvelous, everlasting time together with our Lord Jesus Christ as His Bride, a time impossible to understand, let alone to put into words.

I have chosen various well-known Chistian leaders to listen to as they have proven to be helpful of attention. For such reason, I have them included in my writings.

---

1 E.G. White, *THE GREAT CONTROVERSY*: Celebrating the 500th Anniversary of the Great Protestant Reformation, Remnant Publications, Inc., 2017.

Finally, we may listen to the following words from Dietrich Bonhoeffer who wrote in "Life Together,"

Seek God, not happiness--this is the fundamental rule of all meditation. If you seek God alone, you will gain happiness: that is its promise.

CURRENT
END-TIME DEVELOPMENTS

CHAPTER ONE
ASPECTS OF REPLACEMENT THEOLOGY

Origin of Replacement Theology

Paull Scharf (Comments, Sept. 24, 2021), a Church Ministries Representative in Columbus, Wisconsin, explains the beginning of Replacement Theology by referring to Vlach who suggested that the idea of Replacement Theology started with Origen of Alexandria (185–254), while acknowledging that it was actually "Justin Martyr who became the first person to explicitly identify the church as 'the true spiritual Israel.'"[2]

In Origen's understanding, the only positive function of a physical Israel is that of being a type of spiritual Israel. Diprose then delivers the following synopsis, taking us up to Origen:

> An attitude of contempt toward Israel had become the rule by Origen's time.... In Origen's understanding, the only positive function of physical Israel is that of being a type of spiritual Israel. The promises were not made to physical Israel because she was unworthy of them and incapable of understanding them. Thus, Origen effectively disinherits physical Israel.[8]
> [8] Diprose, p. 84)

According to Diprose, Origen "considers" "the Church ... to be the true Israel."[9] Diprose sums up as follows:

---

[2] Vlach, p. 190. Larry D. Pettegrew concurs with this conclusion regarding Justin Martyr. See "The Curious Case of the Church Fathers and Israel," in *Forsaking Israel: How It Happened and Why It Matters*, ed. Larry D. Pettegrew (The Woodlands, TX: Kress Biblical Resources, 2020), p. 32).

Origen's contribution to replacement theology is particularly incisive, because of his exegetical prowess and because he was the first Christian writer to attempt making a complete statement of the Christian faith…. Thus, for churchmen who read his commentaries and homilies during subsequent centuries, the idea that true Israel had always been the Church appeared to be something taught by the Bible itself.[10]

Diprose, (p. 87)
This stream of thinking persisted until the days of Augustine in the fourth and fifth centuries. What was it that Augustine believed and taught? Well, Burggraff explains:

Not only did he reject a literal 1000-year kingdom on the earth after Jesus' Second Coming, he, like the church fathers before him, erased national Israel from prophecy.[13] [13] Burggraff, p. 71).

Regarding the beginning of Replacement Theology, Vlach suggests that it commenced officially "in the middle of the second century AD," when "Justin Martyr became the first person to explicitly identify the church as 'the true spiritual Israel.'"[4]

Essentials of Replacement Theology
As an introduction to the important subject of Replacement theology, we may take note of the following conversation by Rev. Malcolm Hedding, the former Executive Director of the International Christian Embassy Jerusalem.

Replacement theology rests chiefly on the idea that the whole, or part of the Abrahamic Covenant, has been abolished, for it is this Covenant that promises to Israel eternal ownership of the land of Canaan according to Genesis 17:7-8. This theology concludes that this 'promise' has been removed, and that the restoration of Israel means nothing, as her only hope is in the Church. It must also be made clear that only in Christ Jesus can there be salvation for Jews and Gentiles alike (Romans 1:16-17).

However, I (Peter), among others, do no longer believe that the promise of God in the Abrahamic Covenant concerning the land of Canaan to Israel has been removed, and therefore Israel's modern restoration to the land of Canaan is indeed the fulfillment of Scriptures.

[4] Vlach, p. 190. Larry D. Pettegrew concurs with this conclusion regarding Justin Martyr. See "The Curious Case of the Church Fathers and Israel," in *Forsaking Israel: How It Happened and Why It Matters*, ed. Larry D. Pettegrew (The Woodlands, TX: Kress Biblical Resources, 2020), p. 32.

However, I (Peter), among others, do no longer believe that the promise of God in the Abrahamic Covenant concerning the land of Canaan to Israel has been removed, and therefore Israel's modern restoration to the land of Canaan is indeed the fulfillment of that promise and constitutes a milestone on her 'way home' to her Messiah (Ezekiel 36:24-28).

Rejection of Replacement Theology
Following are highlights taken from Rev. Hedding's explanation why he rejects Replacement Theology advocated by the Abolitionists and the so-called Reconstruction Camp:

1. The Abolitionists
This camp sees the Covenant with Abraham being entirely abolished. However they have serious difficulties, because Paul's writing to the Galatians states that Jesus died in order to bring to our lives the blessings of the Abrahamic Covenant and if we belong to Jesus, we are Abraham's children according to the promise (Galatians 3:13-14, 29)…the writer of the Book of Hebrews states that we can trust God to be faithful to the New Covenant, because He has always been faithful to the Abrahamic Covenant (Hebrews 6:13-20). This reality constitutes a serious problem for the Abolitionists because, if the Abrahamic Covenant has been abolished, then God is a liar and indeed is not faithful, though the writer of Hebrews affirms that He is!

2. Reconstructionist Camp

This theory states that the Abrahamic Covenant has not been abolished but reconstructed. That is, the part that promises land to Israel now means spiritual promises and not literal ones. The problem with this theory is that it is a complete presupposition, and the Scriptures nowhere affirm it. That all nations would be blessed in Christ was the intention of the Abrahamic Covenant from the very beginning, but this does not remove from the Jewish people a national destiny in the Holy Land within the Middle East.

In Ezekiel 36:24-32 we read that Ezekiel teaches the very opposite of Replacement theology, in that Israel's rebellion and sin has not led to land forfeiture, but to judgment and correction. Yet, in the end God will, for His Name's sake, restore Israel to her ancient land and to Himself...The apostle Peter (2 Peter 3:10-13) affirms that there must be a time of "restoration of all things" before Messiah returns. This "restoration of all things" is spoken about by all the prophets - meaning a final regathering to the Land of Canaan and repentance leading to salvation in Jesus. (Amos 9:11-15; Jeremiah 36:26-28).

Israel has always been God's vehicle of world redemption (Romans 9:1-5). Jesus will return to Zion as the root and offspring of David (Revelation 22:1-6; Psalm 2:1-12; Psalm 72:5-11). Replacement theology is thus an instrument of the powers of darkness to frustrate the purpose of God, by disconnecting the Church from this final great redemptive initiative in history.

The heading of a paper entitled, "6 reasons why Replacement Theology is false, and that the Church has not at all replaced the nation of Israel in God's Plan," draws immediate attention to the following quote of Charles Haddon Spurgeon,

> I think we do not attach sufficient importance to the restoration of the Jews. We do not think enough of it. But certainly, if there is anything promised in the Bible it is this.[3]

---

[3] Spurgeon, "The Church of Christ," NPSP 1:213-14. Can be accessed online at the website entitled "The Spurgeon Archives," http//www. Spurgeon.org/misc/eschat2.htm#note55 (accessed May 19, 2012).

In a follow-up to Spurgeon's above-quoted observation, we may listen carefully to what the LORD told Abram before he was to set out on his journey to a land he was going to be led to in faith and obedience:

Genesis 12,

> I will make you into a great nation and I will bless you.
>> I will make your name great, and you will be a blessing.
>> **I will bless those who bless you, and whoever curses you I will curse**; and all peoples on earth will be blessed through you. (Gen. 12:2-3).

John 1,

> There came a man who was sent from God; his name was John. He came as a witness to testify concerning that light, so that through him all men might believe. He himself was not the light; he came only as a witness to the light. The true light that gives light to every man was coming into the world. He was in the world, and though the world was made through him, the world did not recognize him. He came to that which was his own, but his own did not receive him. Yet to all who received him, to those who believed in his name, he gave the right to become children of God, children born not of natural descent, nor of human decision or a husband's will, but born of God. (John 1:6-13).

These two above-noted Bible passages, one from the Old Testament and one from the New, provide a solid biblical rebuttal of Replacement Theology is a most unbiblical conclusion. These two Bible passages are fundamental for a correct understanding of God's lasting support for His original and lasting covenant people, despite of their past three captivities, see below.

Next to this fundamental truth regarding God's original covenant people, the Jews, we have another fundamental and lasting truth regarding the Gentiles, described as follows in Genesis 12,

I will bless those who bless you, and whoever curses you I will curse. (Gen. 12:3).

From 'A Commentary by Gerhard von Rad,' we hear that the following three New Testament references underline that divine promise expressed in the above highlighted sentence, including:
Acts 3,

And you are heirs of the prophets and of the covenant God made with your fathers. He said to Abraham, 'Through your offspring all peoples on earth will be blessed. (Acts 3:25).

Romans 4,
It was not through law that Abraham and his offspring received the promise that he would be heir of the world, but through the righteousness that comes by faith…Therefore, the promise comes by faith, so that it may be by grace and may be guaranteed to all Abraham's offspring— not only to those who are of the law but also to those who are of the faith of Abraham. He is the father of us. As it is written I have made you a father of many nations… (Rom. 4:13, 16-17a).
Galatians 3,
The Scripture foresaw that God would justify the Gentiles by faith and announced the gospel in advance to Abraham: "All nations will be blessed through you." So those who have faith are blessed along with Abraham, the man of faith…The promises were spoken to Abraham and to his seed. The Scripture does not say "and to seeds," meaning many people, but and to your seed," meaning one person, who is Christ.
(Gal. 3:8, 16).
As well-known theologians, Charles H. Spurgeon and Walter C. Kaiser defend the theological position that Jews have returned and continue to return to their biblical, God-given homeland in the Middle East since 1948, 3 years after the ending of WWII in 1945. That return, while still going on, has often been regarded as a highly unexpected, if not miraculous event.

Following is an overview of the return of Jews from three successive captivities/exiles to their God-given territory in the Middle East:

First captivity/exile: The Assyrian Captivity/Exile: 722 BCE – 563 BCE?
    Second captivity/exile: The Babylonian Captivity/Exile: 598 BCE – 538 BCE.
    Third captivity/exile: The World-wide Captivity/Exile: AD 70 – AD 1948.

Note: Many voices speak only of the last two captivities. That means that The Babylonian Captivity is regarded as the first captivity, rather than the Assyrian Captivity.

The Danger of Replacing Israel

Paul Scharf, a Church Ministries Representative in Columbus, Wisconsin, wrote in his blog of September 24, 2012, the following observations concerning attempts to deny the reality of Israel's existence since 1948, and its central place in the world,

As Bible-believing Christians, we must maintain a keen focus on the importance of Israel—from its biblical past, through its strategic present, to its prophetic future…we must always remember that God still has a future for Israel!

Scharf pursues the argument that the tendency to replace Israel (counting the church as the *new Israel* or the *spiritual Israel*, or otherwise taking the concept of Israel (the people, the nation or the land) in some non-literal senseis still prevalent in our time. But it's not a new concept by any stretch of the imagination.

When we replace Israel theologically…at least two negative things begin to happen: First, if we succumb to the errors of Replacement Theology, we will dull our consciences to the imperative of understanding and transmitting the gospel "for the Jew first" (Romans 1:16). Secondly, we will ultimately blur our senses to the immense importance of Israel in its prophetic future, as God has revealed in the Bible. When we replace

Israel, we miss the true, literal intent of the inspired author and minimize its biblical importance in every way.

R. Scott Clark, responding to the question: "Has the Church Replaced Israel?" said,

> I think the best understanding of Romans 9-11 is that God will save all His elect, both Jew and Gentile by *grace* alone, through *faith* alone, in *Christ* alone. He has added Gentiles to the people of God, and He continues to save elect Jews. Perhaps there will be a great future ingathering of Jews to faith in Christ. This is a matter of debate (and future, as we also listen to and take note of the ministry of the Messianic Jews; addition mine). (Note next page).

Note: Read R. Scott Clark on Supersessionism.

The Reformed, however, explained the law as the covenant of works and the gospel as a covenant of grace and sanctification as the natural, necessary consequence of the gospel and grace. In other words, for the Reformed covenant theology it is a way of articulating the gospel of justification by grace alone, through faith alone.

All true churches, i.e. all true Christians, are Messianic, i.e. that all Christians confess Jesus as the Messiah, but I take it that you're referring to Jewish-Christian congregations who retain resurrected believers in Christ, meeting up with believers who are still alive at that time. (Rev. 21: 1-80).

Some aspects of old-covenant practices. My (Peter's) impression is that many such congregations have roots in Dispensationalism and that theology does not account adequately for Paul's teaching in Ephesians 2 that, in Christ, the dividing wall has been broken down and that, in Christ, there is no Jew or Gentile etc. (Gal 3:28; Col 3:11).

It has been widely held by Reformed theologians, since the 16th and 17th centuries, that there will be a future mass conversion of Jews. Not all Reformed theologians hold this view, but it has widely been taught and held.[4] August 21, 2013.

Incorrect Notion of Replacement Theology

The heading of a paper entitled, "6 reasons why Replacement Theology is false, and the Church has not at all replaced the nation of Israel in God's Plan," draws our attention to the following quote of Charles Haddon Spurgeon,

> I think we do not attach sufficient importance to the restoration of the Jews. We do not think enough of it. But certainly, if there is anything promised in the Bible it is this.[5]

Walter C. Kaiser, Jr., informs us that,

> To argue that God replaced Israel with the church is to depart from an enormous body of biblical evidence.[6]

Considering the two above quoted comments we may listen to what the LORD told Abram before he was to set out on his journey to a land he was going to be led to in faith and obedience.

Genesis 12:2-3,

> I will make you into a great nation and I will bless you;
>   I will make your name great, and you will be a blessing.

---

[4] R. Scott Clark is the President of the Heidelberg Reformation Association, the author and editor of, and contributor to several books and the author of many articles. He has taught church history and historical theology since 1997 at Westminster Seminary California. He has also taught at Wheaton College, Reformed Theological Seminary, and Concordia University.

[5] Spurgeon, "The Church of Christ," NPSP 1:213-14. Can be accessed on line at the website entitled "The Spurgeon Archives," http//www. Spurgeon.org/misc/eschat2.htm#note55 (accessed May 19, 2012).

[6] Walter C. Kaiser, "An Evangelical Response," in *Dispensationalism, Israel and the Church: The Search for Definition, ed. C.A. Blaising and D.L. Bock (Grand Rapids: Zondervan, 1992), 364.*

I will bless those who bless you, and whoever curses you I will curse; and all peoples on earth will be blessed through you. (NIV)

John 1,

There came a man who was sent from God; *his name was* John. He came as a witness to testify concerning that light, so that through Him all men might believe. He Himself was not the light; he came only as a witness to the light. The true light that gives light to every man was coming into the world. He was in the world, and though the world was made through Him, the world did not recognize Him. He came to that which was His own, but His own did not receive Him. Yet to all who received Him, to those who believed in His name, He gave the right to become children of God, children born not of natural descent, nor of human decision or a husband's will, but born of God. (Jn. 1:6-13).

The above two passages, one from the Old Testament and one from the New Testament, provide a solid biblical rebuttal of Replacement Theology. These two quoted Bible passages are fundamental for a correct understanding of God's lasting support for His original and lasting covenant people, despite of their past three captivities, see below.

Following this fundamental truth regarding God's *original* covenant people, the Jews, we have another fundamental and lasting truth regarding the Gentiles, described as follows in Genesis 12,

I will bless those who bless you, and whoever curses you I will curse. (Gen. 12:3).

From 'A Commentary by Gerhard von Rad' we hear that the following three New Testament references underline that promise expressed in the above highlighted sentence, including:

And you are heirs of the prophets and of the covenant God made with your fathers. He said to Abraham, 'Through your offspring all peoples on earth will be blessed. (Ac. 3:25).

Romans 4,

It was not through law that Abraham and his offspring received the promise that he would be heir of the world, but through the righteousness that comes by faith…Therefore, the promise comes by faith, so that it may be by grace and may be guaranteed to all Abraham's offspring—not only to those who are of the law but also to those who are of the faith of Abraham. He is the father of us. As it is written,

I have made you a father of many nations… (Rom. 4:13, 16-17a).

Galatians 3,

The Scripture foresaw that God would justify the Gentiles by faith and announced the gospel in advance to Abraham: "All nations will be blessed through you." So those who have faith are blessed along with Abraham, the man of faith…The promises were spoken to Abraham and to his seed. The Scripture does not say "and to seeds," meaning many people, but and to your seed," meaning one person, who is Christ. (Gal. 3:8, 16).

Both well-known theologians, Charles H. Spurgeon and Walter C. Kaiser, defend the theological position that the Jews have been returning and continue to return to their biblical, God-given homeland in the Middle East since 1948, 3 years after the ending of WW II in 1945. That return, while still going on, has often been regarded as a highly unexpected, if not miraculous event.

REFORMED THEOLOGY IS COVENANT THEOLOGY
According to Dr. Richard Pratt: Reformed theology is often associated with "Covenant theology." If you listen carefully, you'll often hear pastors and teachers describe themselves as "Reformed and covenantal."

The terms *reformed* and *covenant* are used together so widely that it helps us to understand why they are connected.

Covenant theology refers to one of the basic beliefs that Calvinists have held about the Bible. All Protestants who have remained faithful to their heritage affirm *sola Scriptura*, the belief that the Bible is our supreme and unquestionable authority. Covenant theology, however, distinguishes the Reformed view of Scripture from other Protestant outlooks by emphasizing that divine covenants unify the teachings of the entire Bible.

Earlier developments in the Reformed, covenantal understanding of Scripture reached a high point in seventeenth-century England with the Westminster Confession of Faith (1646), the Savoy Declaration (1658), the London Baptist Confession of 1689, and each representing different groups of English-speaking Calvinists. With only slight variations among them, these documents each devote an entire chapter to the way God's covenants with humanity reveal the unity of all that the Bible teaches.

For example, the Westminster Confession of Faith speaks of God condescending to reveal Himself to humanity by means of covenant. It then divides the entire history of the Bible into just two covenants: the "Covenant of Works" in Adam and the "Covenant of Grace" in Christ. The Covenant of Works was God's arrangement with Adam and Eve before their fall into sin. The Covenant of Grace governed the rest of the Bible. In this view, all stages of the Covenant of Grace were the same in substance. They differed only as God administered His one Covenant of Grace in Christ in various ways throughout biblical history.

Along these same lines, several more recent Reformed theologians have affirmed the covenantal unity of Scripture by relating biblical covenants to what the New Testament calls "the kingdom of God." Jesus indicated the importance of God's kingdom in the opening words of the Lord's Prayer:

> Our Father in heaven, hallowed be Your name. Your kingdom come, Your will be done on earth as it is in heaven. (Matt. 6:9–10)).

Jesus' words indicate that the foremost goal of history is the glory and honor of God Himself.

Covenant theology has enabled Reformed theologians to see that the New Testament is quite similar to the Old Testament in the following three areas: works and grace, corporate and individual faith, and earthly and spiritual concerns… At the same time, there is also a growing need for covenant theology to be strongly reaffirmed in contemporary Reformed circles. However, in recent decades, many newer advocates of Reformed theology have neglected Covenant theology.

Note:

"Reformed theology is Covenant theology."

Dr. Richard L. Pratt Jr. is the founder and president of Third Millennium Ministries and is also an adjunct professor at Reformed Theological Seminary in Orlando, Fla.

COVENANT THEOLOGY IS NOT REPLACEMENT THEOLOGY

The Source of Replacement Theology (Supersession)

The source of Replacement Theology came about in the first century. The Messianic/Christian debt to Hebrew Scripture, both Jewish exegesis and divine revelation, were evident to all followers of The Way. In fact, Jewish-Christian relations, despite second and third century Christian elitist assaults upon all things Jewish, continued with good rhythm and solid relationship until the mid-fourth century with the advent of the First Council of Nicaea. At this Council meeting, under Constantine's oversight, the Church formally disconnected from the Jewish roots of Christian theology and practice by separating the celebration of Easter from the Celebration of Passover.

However, the sentiments of the Bishops at Nicaea have their foundations in debates that began in the second century. Justin Martyr crafted his Dialogue with Trypho the Jew on the heels of the Bar Kochba uprising in the Land of Israel, then under Roman rule, and first called "Palestine," in 135 C.E. The Dialogue was finally published in 150 C.E. some 15 years before Justin's martyrdom. Here Justin made his strong case for a "New Israel," a "True Israel," in replacement of biblical Israel—hence, the term "Replacement Theology," or "Super-secessionism," i.e. that the Church supersedes Israel.

The Church fathers sought to create a new "wall of partition" between Jewish and Christian people. The natural affinity Jews and Christians, enjoyed in the second and third centuries, alarmed the Church fathers who borrowed from both Justin and Marcion to support an anti-Judaic Christian theology of Israel. This would not only result in thousands of assaults upon Jewish people over the next 1,500 years or so, but also cripple Christian self-understanding as a "daughter" of the Faith of Israel.

Martin Luther and other reformers inherited this anti-Jewish theological posture and cultural prejudice. Luther, credited for his emphasis on justification by faith, took severe liberties to castigate the Jewish people, even Jewish believers in Yeshua. His instilled cultural dread of Jews and all things Jewish pushed him into presuming that newly established European Protestantism was at risk of being fully swallowed up by massive Christian conversion to Judaism. This led Luther to craft, during the final decade of his life, a horrific written sermonic siege upon the Jewish world. His expressions of anti-Semitism have been often quoted by the Nazi Regime in the days of Hitler.

However, the re-establishment of the Land of Israel in 1948, and the recapture of the City of Jerusalem in 1967, have forced the Church to reconsider long-held attitudes towards the Jewish people. With the nation re-born in a day (Isaiah 66:7-8) and the City of Jerusalem now under Israeli sovereignty (Luke 21:24), Christians of many denominations are seriously reconsidering many long-held theological positions concerning Israel and the Jewish people, including myself. May the Lord eradicate the fallacy of Replacement Theology from His Bride, the Church, in our lifetime and in our days!

Source: By Gateway Center for Israel.

Many scholars conclude that Hitler's violent antisemitism was enabled by a wake of anti-Jewish theologies of church heroes like Calvin and Luther. Living in a post-Holocaust world, it is difficult for modern Christians to believe that antisemitism was flowing in the lifeblood of the Church for thousands of years. Yet, it did. Why? John Calvin's answer,

Their rotten and unbending stiff-neckedness deserves that they
be oppressed unendingly and without measure or end and that
they die in their misery without the pity of anyone.

For many followers of Jesus, this type of glaring antisemitism comes
as an alarming surprise. How could one of the most respected theologians in Christian tradition spout off something so toxic? Others might
wonder if I (Peter) am simply framing Calvin unfairly, taking his quote
out of context. With that in mind, here's one of the many quotes of
Calvin's contemporaries – Luther.
Martin Luther:

Set fire to their synagogues or schools and bury and cover with
dirt whatever will not burn, so that no man will ever again see
a stone or cinder of them. This is to be done in honor of our
Lord and of Christendom, so that God might see that we are
Christians. (Source: Jewish Virtual Library.)

At the beginning of his career, Martin Luther was apparently sympathetic to Jewish resistance to the Catholic Church. However, he expected the Jews to convert to his purified Christianity; when they did
not, he turned violently against them…Luther used violent and vulgar
language throughout his career. While we do not expect religious figures
to use this sort of language in the modern world, it was not uncommon
in the early 16th century.
Source: Luther's work entitled, 'The Jews & their Lies.'

CHAPTER TWO

ISRAEL'S SUFFERINGS AND FINAL RETURN TO HER
HOMELAND

Brief overview of how God led Israel to their God-given land in the Middle East

Following are O.T. Bible verses that speak about God's promise to lead the Israelites into the land He had promised them to inherit for ever:

Genesis 12,

1 The LORD had said to Abram, 'Leave your country, your people and your father's household and go to the land I will show you. 2 I will make you into a great nation and I will bless you; I will make your name great, and you will be a blessing. 3 I will bless those who bless you. And whoever curses you I will curse; and all peoples on earth will be blessed through you. (Gen. 12:1-3).

Exodus 3,

7 The LORD said (to Moses), "I have indeed seen the misery of My people...8 So I have come down to rescue them from the hand of the Egyptians and to bring them up out of that land into a good and spacious land, a land flowing with milk and honey—the home of the Canaanites, Hittites, Amorites, Perizzites, Hivites and Jebusites. (Ex. 3:7-8).

Leviticus 23,

9 The LORD said to Moses, 10 'Speak to the Israelites and say to them: 'When you enter the land I am going to give you and you reap its harvest, bring to the priest a sheaf of the first grain you harvest. (Lev. 23:9-10).

Numbers 32,

6 Moses said to the Gadites and Reubenites, shall your countrymen go to war while you sit here? 7 Why do you discourage the Israelites from going over into the land the LORD has given them? (Numbers. 32:6-7).

Deuteronomy 7,

6b The LORD your God has chosen you out of all the peoples on the face of the earth to be His people, His treasure possession... 8 ...because the Lord loved you and kept the oath He swore to your forefathers that He brought you out with a mighty hand and redeemed you from the land of slavery, from the power of Pharaoh king of Egypt. (Deut. 7:6b, 8).

Deuteronomy 31,

14 The LORD said to Moses *write down for yourselves* this song (see Deut. 32) and teach it to the Israelites and have them sing it, so that it may be a witness for Me against them. 20 When I have brought them into the land flowing with milk and honey. The land I promised on oath to their forefathers... (Deut. 31:14a, 19-20a).

Joshua 1,

1 After the death of Moses …the LORD said to Joshua, son of Nun, Moses' aid: 2 'Moses My servant is dead. Now then, you and all these people, get ready to cross the Jordan River into the land I am about to give to them—to the Israelites….4 Your territory will extend from the desert to Lebanon, and from the great river, the Euphrates—all the Hittite country—to the Great Sea on the west…I will never leave you nor forsake you…

7 Be strong and very courageous. Be careful to obey all the law My servant Moses gave you; do not turn away from it to the right or to the left, that you may be successful wherever you go…Three days from now you will cross the Jordan here to go in and take possession of the land the Lord your God is giving for your own. (Josh. 1: 1, 2, 4, 7, 11b).

Joshua 3,

14 When the people broke camp to cross the Jordan, the priests carrying the ark of the covenant went ahead of them. 15 Now the Jordan is at flood stage all during harvest. Yet as touched the water's edge 16 the water from upstream stopped flowing. It piled up in a heap soon as the priests who carried the ark of the LORD reached the Jordan and their feet a great distance away…while the water flowing down to the Sea of the Arabah (the Salt Sea) was completely cut off. So the people crossed over opposite Jericho. (Josh. 3:14-17).

Joshua 9,

1 When all the kings west of the Jordan heard about these things—those in the hill country, in the western foothills, and along the entire coast of the Great Sea as far as Lebanon (the kings of the Hittites, Amorites, Canaanites, Perizzites, Hivites

and Jebusites)—2 they came together to make war against Joshua and Israel. (Josh. 9:1-2).

Joshua 10,

12 On the day the LORD gave the Amorites over to Israel, Joshua said to the LORD in the presence of Israel: 13 So the sun stood still, and the moon stopped, till the nation avenged itself on its enemies, as it is written in the Book of Jashar. The sun stopped in the middle of the sky and delayed going down about a full day. 14 There has never been a day like it before or since, a day when the LORD was fighting for Israel! (Josh. 10:12-14).

Impressions of Israel's Sufferings

From 'The Friends of Israel Gospel Ministries, Inc.': 'ISRAEL MY GLORY,'

In the November/December 2022 edition, p.30, Cameron Joyner speaks of Israel's suffering as spoken by Moses, warning them about the consequences of their disobedience as follows:

I will turn your cities into ruins and lay waste your sanctuaries, and I will take no delight in the pleasing aroma of your offerings. I will lay waste the land, so that your enemies who live there will be appalled. I will scatter you among the nations and will draw out my sword and pursue you. Your land will be laid waste, and your cities will lie in ruin. (Lev. 26:31-33).

Then, in the January/February 2023 edition, p.21, Bruce Scott reminds us of a similar divine warning for His people in the following way:

Just as it pleased the LORD to make you prosper and increase in number, so it will please Him to ruin and destroy you. You will be uprooted from the land you are entering to possess. Then the

LORD will scatter you among all nations, from one end of the earth to the other. There you will worship other gods...Among those nations you will find no repose, no resting place for the sole of your foot. There the LORD will give you an anxious mind, eyes weary with longing, and a despairing heart. You will live in constant suspense, filled with dread both night and day, never sure of your life. (Deut. 28:63-66).

Scott then commented,

That scattering of God's people, the Jews, happened in AD 70 when the Romans destroyed the Second Temple...Jewish people were expelled from cities and kingdoms throughout medieval "Christian Europe," including Germany, Austria, Hungary, the papal States, as well as Italy and Spain, following the Alhambra Decree (Edict of Expulsion) including the following three possibilities:

(1) Convert to Catholicism,

(2) Keep their Jewish faith, but losing all they owned, or

(3) Remain Jewish, stay in Spain, and be killed. Tens of thousands converted and several hundred thousand left.

Destruction of Jerusalem and the Temple AD 70

Before we move on to more information of Israel's suffering since AD 70, we may pause and reflect on the years leading up to AD 70. It is of interest to listen to Hanegraaff's understanding of that period as described in his famous "Olivet Discourse," Matt. 24,

Jesus shared just with His disciples. But prior to that discourse I want to draw attention to what Jesus said to the crowds and His disciples we read about in Matthew 23. In this chapter Jesus, very publicly, admonished the teachers of the law and the Pharisees. He repeatedly accused them as being hypocrites, blind guides and brood of vipers thereby explaining why he called them that way.

At the end of that explosive public accusation of those spiritual leaders, Jesus said, while addressing to those spiritual leaders,

35 And so upon you will come all the righteous blood that has been shed on earth, from the blood of righteousness Abel to the blood of Zechariah son of Berekiah, whom you murdered between the temple and the altar. 36 I tell you the truth, all this will come upon this generation. (Matt. 23:35-36).

Before commenting on these verses, Hanegraaff quoted Dr. Kenneth Gentry who commented on these verses in the Olivet Discourse as follows,

This generation in view is a non-apocalypse, non-poetic, unambiguous, didactic assertion.[7]

Hanegraaff then continued to explain that,

This generation" appears with surprising regularity in the Gospels, and it always applies to Jesus' contemporaries. In Matthew 11, Jesus asks, "To what can I compare this generation" (v. 16). Here, as in every other usage of this phrase, the generation in view is the very generation that rejected the incarnate Christ who performed miracles in their midst.[8] The reference to "this generation" refers to the then-present generation, not to a generation that is alive in 1948. p.79.

Then, not long after, Jesus, pointing to the temple, explained to His disciples,

2 I tell you the truth, not one stone here will be left on another, every stone will be thrown down. (Matt. 24:2).

With Hanegraaff, we need to realize that those disciples of Jesus had, at that moment, no inkling of a coming destruction of their Temple

---

[7] According to a standard New Testament Greek Lexicon: *this*, in Matthew 24:34, is referring to something comparatively near at hand, p. 250.
[8] Hank Hanegraaff, THE APOCALYPSE CODE, Thomas Nelson, Nashville, Tennessee, 2007, p.77

by Roman soldiers years later in AD 70. So, they asked Jesus when he expected such a serious destruction was going to happen. Placing ourselves in the shoes of those disciples we only can imagine how difficult it must have been for those brothers in Christ to really understand the answer Jesus gave them in the following verses, Matt. 24:4-15, to begin with.

It must have been quite puzzling for those disciples to understand what Jesus was telling them about future fearful, mind-boggling, even shattering events. What they heard Jesus saying was a mixture of terrifying events that could take place rather soon, as well as in a farther future. One thing was sure, there was a time coming in which there would be much human suffering. Another thing we may learn from Jesus' prediction regarding future events is that certain events could already take place around the time the Romans would create immense havoc, destruction and great human casualties around AD 70.

This is noticeable when we hear that Jesus more than once said, "then you" or "when you" to His disciples, while He also could speak to future generations about terrible events taking place in later years. However, Hanegraaff's opinion is that Jesus spoke to His disciples about terrible future developments in a way that only could be understood by His disciples as events they themselves would experience.[9] That would include that the temple would be so totally destroyed that "*Not one stone will be left on another; everyone will be thrown down,*" (Matt. 24:2).

In the same Olivet Discourse, we read the following words, also spoken by Jesus,

> 29 Immediately after the distress of those days, 'the sun will be darkened, and the moon will not give its light; the stars will fall from the sky, and the heavenly bodies will be shaken. (Matt. 24:29).

Hanegraaff's explanation of Jesus's words, spoken in the above-quoted verse in Matt. 24, are judgment metaphors similarly used in Isaiah 13,

---

[9] Hank Hanegraaff, THE APOCALYPSE CODE, Thomas Nelson, Nashville, Tennessee, 2007, 77-84.

9 See, the day of the LORD is coming—a cruel day, with wrath and fierce anger—to make the land desolate and destroy the sinners within it. 10 The stars from heaven and their constellations will not show their light. The rising sun will be darkened, and the moon will not give its light. (Isa. 13:9-10).

Furthermore, Hanegraaff's explains that Isaiah used the sun, moon, and stars as judgment metaphors against Babylon, so our Lord used them as judgment images against Jerusalem. But then, one may wonder why we read that Jerusalem was awaiting such a severe judgement from the Roman army. In the Bible book, Revelation, Chapter 17, we read about a woman with the following title written on her forehead,

MYSTERY
BABYLON THE GREAT
THE MOTHER OF PROSTITUTES
AND OF THE ABOMINATION OF THE EARTH[10]

While these words concerning 'Babylon the Great' have been interpreted by many as pointing to the contemporary Roman Catholic Church, Hanegraaff wants us to understand that in biblical history only one nation is inextricably linked to the moniker "harlot, namely Israel!"[11] He makes hereby the biblical connection of the above-described identity of that 'women' in Rev. 17 and the 'woman' described in Ezekiel 17.

At this point we may return to the date of AD 70 and the suffering of Israel under attack by the Roman soldiers and the destruction of Jerusalem with her Temple. We may agree with those who hold on to the fact that the New Testament, most likely, with the exclusion of the book of Revelation, was written prior to AD 70, as there is no report on the contrary except from those who think differently.

It seems that the four Gospels and Paul's many letters have most likely been written prior to AD 70, and thereby nothing has been mentioned about the destruction of the city of Jerusalem and the Temple in

---

[10] Ibid. 118; Rev. 17:5
[11] Ibid. 119

that year. We may assume that John's letter 'Revelation' has been written around AD 90, i.e. after the terrible destruction of Jerusalem and the Temple 20 years earlier. We may then also add that the contents of the Bible have been, most likely, written before AD 70.

The New Testament teaches, that during a period of about 40 years between AD 30 and AD 70, many important events took place. Following the death, resurrection, and ascension of Jesus Christ, the Holy Spirit was poured out on those gathered on Pentecost. (Ac. 2:1-13). We further read about the sharing of possessions among those believers (Ac. 4:32-35), as well as about the persecution of the apostles (Ac. 17-42), the stoning of Stephen (Ac. 7:54-8:1a) followed by the persecution and scattering of those being part of the church at Jerusalem. (Ac. 8b-3).

This period of about 40 years, included Paul's three mission trips during which he was accompanied by his personal physician Dr. Luke, who wrote the Gospel of Luke. During his three mission trips, Paul brought the gospel first to the Jews in their synagogues, then to the Gentiles as well, as we can read in his many NT letters. From his writings, we also understand that, despite much rejection, the contents of these letters were overwhelmingly accepted by many Gentiles.

From then on, the Gospel message was spread throughout the Western world and beyond. We need to realize thereby that all of Jesus' disciples did make their own mission trips outside Israel. We also learn that, like Paul, they too were killed, as we can read in APPENDIX B: '*Where and How Jesus' Apostles Died*,' except for John. From that list we also learn about the various countries that received the Gospel message, including the Soviet Union, Asia Minor, Turkey, Greece, North Africa, Persia, Ethiopia, India, South Arabia.

The importance of the Gospel infiltrating the world beyond Israel's borders is that all those evangelistic activities must have drawn Satan's attention and causing him to stop the progress of the Gospel throughout Europe and other countries. That significant and alarming progress of the Gospel must certainly have urged Satan to figure out how to stop such an intolerable progress.

It could well be that Satan must have been stirring Rome to become his instrument to stop and to punish those missionary efforts and their successes in bringing the Gospel beyond Israel's borders. If so, it could have been possible that Satan had influenced Rome to punish those Jewish efforts to spread the Gospel beyond Israel's borders by destroying Jerusalem and the Temple and taking the lives of thousands of Jews.

We may agree with Hanegraaff's understanding that the letter Revelation, written by John on the island of Patmos, would also have said something about Jerusalem's terrible destruction. Let me quote Hanegraaff's thoughts on this important issue of the time Revelation was written,

> If Revelation is a book that describes what is about to take place in the twenty-first century, it would have been largely irrelevant to first-century Christians. While Revelation is as relevant as Romans to modern-day readers, it was written to seven historical churches living in the shadow of the Neronian persecution. It is in this milieu that Jesus (through John who was at that moment in the Spirit, addition mine) admonished the churches of Asia to stand firm in the conviction that Christ, not Caesar, is both Lord and Savior.

Before leaving that terrible war in AD 70, we may listen, once more, to Hanegraaff's summing up of how Jewish historian Josephus described the horror of that war started by Vespasian and his son Titus, after having first surrounded Jerusalem with a wall, and relegating the Jews within to either starvation or surrender,

> Those who had failed to flee to Pella 'prowled around like mad dogs, gnawing at anything; belts, shoes, and even the leather from their shields." In graphic detail he recounts stories such as that of Mary of Bethezuba. "Maddened by hunger, she seized the infant at her breast and said, 'Poor baby, why should I preserve you for war, famine, and rebellion? Come, be my food—

vengeance against the rebels, and the climax of Jewish tragedy for the world.' With that, she killed her infant son, roasted his body, and devoured half of it, hiding the remainder.

Then, by August, the altar of the temple was littered with heaps of rotting corpses, and "streams of blood flowed down the steps of the sanctuary." And on August 30 the unthinkable happened,

The very day on which the former temple had been destroyed by the king of Babylon," the second temple was set ablaze. As John had prophesied,
In one day, her plagues will overtake her: death, mourning and famine. She will be consumed by fire, for mighty is the Lord God who judges her. (Rev.18:8).

While the temple was in flames, the victors not only stole everything they could lay their hands on, but also slaughtered all who were caught. No pity was shown to age or rank, old men or children, the laity or priests—all were massacred." By September 26, all Jerusalem was in flame. 'The total number of prisoners taken during the war was 97,000 and those who died during the siege 1,100,000.

The following brief article has been derived from a discussion concerning developments leading to the destruction of Jerusalem and the Second Temple.[12]

The First Jewish–Roman War (66–73 CE/AD), sometimes called the Great Jewish Revolt, or The Jewish War, was the first of three major rebellions by the Jews against the Roman Empire fought in Roman-controlled Judea, resulting in the destruction of Jewish towns, the displacement of its people and the appropriation of land for Roman military use, as well as the destruction of the Jewish Temple and polity. The revolt began in AD 66, as the crisis escalated due to anti-taxation protests and clashes between Jews and pagans in mixed cities. The Roman governor, seized money from the Second Temple's treasury and arrested numerous senior Jewish figures.

---

[12] Wikipedia

All that turmoil prompted widespread rebellion in Jerusalem that culminated in the capture of the Roman garrison by rebel forces as the pro-Roman king Herod Agrippa II and Roman officials fled. To quell the unrest, Cestius Gallus, the legate of Syria, brought in the Syrian army, consisting of the Legion XII *Fulminata* and auxiliary troops. Despite initial advances and the conquest of Jaffa, the Syrian Legion was ambushed and defeated by Jewish rebels at the Battle of Beth Horon with 6,000 Romans massacred and the Legion's aquila lost.

In AD 66, a Judean provisional government was formed in Jerusalem led by former High Priest Ananus ben Ananus, Joseph ben Gurion and Joshua ben Gamla. Yosef ben Matityahu (Josephus) was appointed as the rebel commander in Galilee and Eleazar, ben Hanania as the commander in Edom. Later, in Jerusalem, an attempt by Menahem ben Yehuda, leader of the Sicarii, to take control of the city failed. He was executed and the remaining Sicarii were ejected from the city. Simon bar Giora, a peasant leader, was also expelled by the new government.

The siege of Jerusalem in 70 CE was the decisive event of the First Jewish–Roman War (66–73 CE), in which the Roman army led by future emperor Titus besieged Jerusalem, the center of Jewish rebel resistance in the Roman province of Judaea. Following a five-month siege, the Romans destroyed the city and the Second Jewish Temple. The destruction of Jerusalem and the Second Temple marked a major turning point in Jewish history. The loss of mother-city, Jerusalem, and her temple, necessitated a reshaping of Jewish culture to ensure its survival. Many followers of Jesus of Nazareth also survived the city's destruction. They spread his teachings across the Roman Empire, giving rise to the new religion of Christianity.

The Dead Sea Scrolls

When one hears about a report concerning the destruction of Jerusalem in AD 70 and much more destruction around in the country of Israel, as well as hear that much, if not most, of the Biblical contents have been written prior AD 70, including the destruction of the Temple, we may come to the conclusion that the nearly 2000-year old Dead-Sea Scrolls, found in eleven caves near Khirbet Qumran on the northwestern shores of the Dead Sea, were most likely hidden by those escaping that terrible war to prevent that those Scrolls would be found and successively destroyed by the Roman army. It is known that all books of the Bible have been found among the Dead Sea Scroll collection. Notice hereby that the location of where those scrolls have been found is not that far from Jerusalem.

Remembering 'God's Lasting Purpose for Israel

In Scott's overview of various episodes in Israel's wanderings since AD 70, also includes God's retribution of Gentile nations, due to their anti-Semitic treatments of the Jews. He reminds us of this holy judgement in the book of Joel, as part of The Day of the LORD,

> In those days and at that time when I will restore the fortunes of Judah and Jerusalem, I will gather all nations and bring them down to the Valley of Jehoshaphat. There I will enter into judgment against them concerning My inheritance, My people Israel, for they scattered My people among the nations and divided up My land. (Joel 3:1-2).

Satan will war against God until he is cast into the Lake of Fire[13] (Rev. 20:10), but all of Israel will be saved (Zech. 13:8-9; Rom. 11:26-27). Then antisemitism will be a thing of the past (Zech. 8:23). Until that day, we can expect acts of antisemitism, such as Beth Israel faces, to escalate on February 13, 2023. Then another war starting by Hamas on October 7, 2024, ending at the end of 2024.

Les Crawford says, 'Despite man's attempts to destroy the Jewish people and the culture God established among them, God's purpose will not be undone.' p. 19.

However, besides all the talk, predictions and much scorn about the Jewish people, Bruce Scott does not forget to remind us also of the special blessings for Israel, of God's Word that makes repeated predictions for a much better and a wonderful lasting future for His covenant people. Thus, the Jewish people received that divine promise and listened

---

[13] NIV translation speaks of 'lake of burning sulfur.'

to God's wonderful and very uplifting promise articulated in the book Ezekiel, where we read,

> 11 For this is what the Sovereign LORD says: I will search for My sheep and look after them. 12 As a shepherd looks after his scattered flock when he is with them, so will I look after My sheep. I will rescue them from all the places where they were scattered on a day of clouds and darkness. 13 I will bring them out from the nations and gather them from the countries, and I will pasture them on the mountains of Israel, in the ravines and in all the settlements in the land. (Ezek. 34:11-13).

Israel's Second and Final Return to the Middle East

Reading Jonathan Cahn's book, "THE ORACLE" gave me (Peter) enough reason to take a closer look at God's Word, and to write briefly about biblical facts that clearly indicate a final, future return of Jews from all nations to their God-given original homeland.

Following are some fragments of biblical predictions of a future, final return of Jewish people to their homeland.[14]

In the Old-Testament Scripture we read about Israel's initial possession of the land Canaan, located in the Middle East, upon God's direction to Abram to leave the country he lived in, and to go to a land God would show him, as we read in Genesis 12, vs.1. In the next two verses God makes the following significant promises,

> I will make you into a great nation and will bless you; I will make your name great, and you will be a blessing. I will bless those who bless you, and whoever curses you I will curse; and all peoples on earth will be blessed through you. (Gen. 12:2-3).

At this point, we will skip the entire period in which the Israelites were held captive in Egypt, followed by the 40-year period of traveling

---

[14] Jonathan Cahn, "*The Oracle: The Jubilean Mysteries Unveiled*," Frontline, Charisma Media/Charisma House Book Group, Florida, pp. 24-27.

through the desert to the land of Canaan. That entire period is covered in the first five books of the Bible, including Genesis, Exodus, Leviticus, Numbers and Deuteronomy.

Going through the entire history God's people, we read at the very end of the five books of Moses, Deuteronomy, Chapter 34,

> Then Moses climbed Mount Nebo from the plains of Moab to the top of Pisgah, across from Jericho. There the LORD showed him the whole land—from Gilead to Dan, all of Naphtali, the territory of Ephraim and Manasseh, all the land of Judah as far as the western sea, the Negev and the whole region from the Valley of Jericho, the City of Palms, as far as Zoar. Then the LORD said to him, this is the land I promised on oath to Abraham, Isaac and Jacob, when I said, "I will give it to your descendants. (Deut. 34:1-4).

Soon after God spoke those words to Moses, he died, and then God instructed Joshua, the son of Nun, who was Moses aide, with the following words in the Book Joshua,

Moses my servant is dead. Now then, you and all these people, get ready to cross the Jordan River into the land I am about to give them— to the Israelites. I will give you every place where you set your foot, as I promised Moses. Your territory will extend from the desert to Lebanon, and from the great river, the Euphrates—all the Hittite country—to the Great Sea on the west (called these days the Mediterranean Sea…. Be strong and courageous, because you will lead these people to inherit the land I swore to their forefathers to give them. Be strong and very courageous. (Josh. 1:1-4, 6-7a).

It is of great interest to return to Moses' previous book, Deuteronomy, especially Chapter 28, where we read at the end of verse 63, about the prediction that, due to Israel's disobedience, the Lord is going to uproot the Israelites from the land they are about to enter and possess. After having possessed the new land we read in the next verse,

Then the LORD will scatter them among all nations, from one end of the earth to the other. There you will worship other gods---gods of wood and stone, which neither you nor your fathers have known. (Deut. 28:64).

The above quoted words *'from one end of the earth to the other'* indicate that Jews would be dispersed from their God-given homeland in the Middle East into the many countries of the world. That world-wide exile began in the year A.D. 70.[15] That awful event of driving God's covenant people out of their God-given country has been altogether a heinous event, when we also consider how Roman soldiers destroyed Jerusalem.

The above stated divine prediction that the Israelites would be dispersed throughout the world, we also hear in the Bible, several chapters later, about a final return of thousands of Jews from all corners of the world back to their homeland, as we read in book of Deuteronomy, Chapter 30,

1 When all these blessings and curses I have set before you come upon you and you take them to heart wherever the LORD your God disperses you among the nations, 2 and when you and your children return to the LORD your God and obey Him with all your heart and with all your soul according to everything I command you today, 3 then the LORD your God will restore your fortunes and have compassion on you and gather you again from all the nations where He scattered you. 4 Even if you have been banished to the most distant land under heavens, from there the LORD your God will gather you and bring you back. 5 He will bring you to the land that belonged to your fathers, and you will take possession of it. He will make you more prosperous and numerous than your fathers. (Deut. 30:1-5).

There are two other Old Testament passages in the book of Ezekiel, Chapter 34, and Chapter 36 about similar divine promises,

---

[15] Jonathan Cahn, The Oracle,' p.26

11 For this is what the Sovereign LORD says: I Myself will search for My sheep and look after them. 12 As a shepherd looks after his scattered flock when he is with them, so will I look after My sheep. I will rescue them from all the places where they were scattered on a day of clouds and darkness. 13 I will bring them out from the nations and gather them from the countries, and I will bring them into their own land. I will pasture them on the mountains of Israel, in the ravines, and in all settlements in the land. (Ezek. 34:11-13).

Chapter 36,

For I will take you out of the nations; I will gather you from allthe countries and bring you back into your own land. I will sprinkle clean water on you, and you will be clean; I will cleanse you from all your impurities and from all your idols. I will give will give you a new heart and put a new spirit in you; I will remove from your heart of stone and give you a heart of flesh.

And I will put My spirit in you and move you to follow My decrees and be careful to keep my laws. (Ezekiel 36: 24-27).

The beginning of the fulfillment of the above-mentioned divine promises about the return of the many Jews to their homeland occurred in the year 1948. That was three years after WWII had ended. I concur with Cahn that "The official and remarkable return of the Jewish people to their ancient land, beginning in 1948, would be the sign of the dawn of the so- called end times."

Israel: A Separate State and Special Nation

1. Israel's historical development in a nutshell.
From Genesis 12, we learn that the Israelites were originally coming from a Gentile world. Their origin can be traced back to the time Abram received the call from the LORD to leave his country to go a land God

was going to show him. Abram heard the following promise from the LORD,

> I will make you into a great nation and will bless you; I will make your name great. And you will be a blessing. 3 I will bless bless those who bless you, and whoever curses you I will curse; and all peoples on earth will be blessed through you. Genesis 12:2-3.

Abraham got two sons, Isaac and Jacob, who got 12 sons. Jacob's family ended up initially in the land called Canaan. That ancient land of Canaan included territory between the eastern shore of the Mediterranean Sea and west of the Jordan River, which today encompasses modern Lebanon, portions of southern Syria, and Israel. Then, a time of famine led Jacob's sons to Egypt where Joseph, Jacob's youngest son was in charge, though not known to Jacob and his sons. (That is a story all by itself). During the time in Egypt the Israelites, while living and working as slaves to the Egyptians, became very numerous.

During the many years in Egypt Moses was born and who became the leader of the Israelites. Frictions between the Israelites and Egypt's leader, Pharaoh, led God to send many different plagues to Egypt that eventually led Pharaoh to have Israel leave the country under the leadership of Moses. That departure became known as the Exodus from Egypt to the land God had promised the Israelites has begun.

During the following period of 40 years, God led His chosen people, while hearing various divine stipulations and many human acts of disobedience to God, arrive finally near the land the Lord had promised on oath to Abraham. In Deuteronomy 34: 1-4 we read that the LORD showed Moses, (while standing on the top of Pisgah after climbing Mount Nebo, east of the Jordan River and across from Jericho), the land they were about to enter. Then the Lord described to Moses that land as follows,

> Your territory will extend from the desert to Lebanon, and from the great river, the Euphrates—all the Hittite country—to the

Great Sea on the west (i.e. the Mediterranean Sea). No one will be able to stand up against you all the days of your life…

6 Be strong and courageous, because you will lead these people to inherit the land I swore to their forefathers to give them. 7 Be strong and courageous…9 Joshua said to the Israelites, "Come here and listen to the words of the LORD your God…10b he will certainly drive out before you the Canaanites, Hittites, Hivites, Perizzites, Girgashites, Amorites and Jebusites" 16 So the people crossed over opposite Jericho Joshua. (Deut. 1:6-7a; 3:9-10b, 16c).

2. Israel's present position

It will be helpful to develop a biblical view of Israel in terms of her recent past and present position in the Middle East. We gain helpful understanding of Israel's position in the Middle East by hearing Soeren Kern on some of her history on Jerusalem's Temple Mount.[16] Kern's response was since this resolution calls Jerusalem's Temple Mount by its Muslim name only. He thereby expressed his concern that the UN General Assembly's intention has most likely been to treat the so-called Jerusalem Resolution as being part of Islam's effort to erase Jewish history and rebrand that historic site as exclusively Islamic.

The Temple Mount, being the holiest site in Judaism, includes the Dome of the Rock (AD 705) and the al-Aqsa mosque (AD 705). It occupies the site of the ancient Jewish Temple King Solomon completed in 957 BC. The Jewish presence there dates back some 3,000 years, predating the Islamic presence by 1,700 years! It is interesting to know that Jerusalem appears 806 times in the Bible: 660 times in the O.T. and 146 times in the N.T.[17] By contrast, Islam's Qur'an never mentions Jerusalem.[18]

It is no wonder why Israelites are upset about the decision made by the UN General Assembly favoring Muslims by calling Jerusalem's

---

[16] Soeren Kern, 'UN REWRITES TEMPLE-MOUNT HISTORY,' magazine 'ISRAEL MY GLORY, 7, March/April, 2022.

[17] Baker's Bible Dictionary.

[18] Soeren Kern, 'UN REWRITES TEMPLE-MPUNT HISTORY,' magazine 'ISRAEL MY GLORY, 7, March/April, 2022.

Temple Mount by its Muslim name only. That favoritism becomes even more suspicious when we realize that Jerusalem was founded in 3,000 BC, predating Islam by 3,600 years; and then also realizing that that Muslim interest in the city has waxed and waned. Besides that, Jerusalem 'became the focus of religious and political Arab activity only at the beginning of the twentieth century.'

It is understandable that Israel's permanent representative to the UN, Gilad Erdan, in response to that very suspicious declaration, spoke of "The hypocrisy of these resolutions being truly outrageous," as it is "A resolution about Jerusalem that does not refer to its ancient roots is not an ignorant mistake, but an attempt to distort and rewrite history!"

Christopher Smith states that all three above-mentioned millennial views do agree that God's plan for the Israelites was and, as I (Peter) understand, continues to draw them (referred to as Messianic Jews) into the multinational community of Jesus' followers that constitutes the people of God. Both, believing Jews and Gentiles, as followers of Jesus Christ, are the ones who are part of the One Church of Jesus Christ that continues to grow.

Smith refers to *dispensationalism*, a theological position promoted by John Nelson Darby (1830s), as he expected a *Jewish* millennium on earth during which Christ would reign for a thousand years as the king of the Jews. This is apparently the understanding of Dispensational pre-millennialists. Smith reminds us that such an understanding differed from a *Christian* millennium, in which Christ's reign over the multinational community of His followers (already a present spiritual reality) would be extended over the whole world.' However, according to Smith, they differ from traditional premillennialists, who, like postmillennialists and a-millennialists, have always expected a Christian millennium, in which the Jews are drawn into the multinational community of Jesus' followers.

When Smith speaks here of a Christian millennialism, I (Peter) was reminded of Jonathan Cahn's book, '*The Return of the gods*' in which he speaks of three different stages in world history: a pre-Christian, a Christian and a post-Christian civilization subsequently. He speaks of the differences between pre-and post-Christian societies as follows:

A pre-Christian civilization may produce a Caligula, or a Nero. But a post-Christian civilization will produce a Stalin or a Hitler.

A pre-Christian society may give birth to barbarity. But a post-Christian society will give birth to even darker offspring, including Fascism, Communism, and Nazism.

It seems that with the beginning of the New Testament period we began the so-called Christian society, also referred to as the Christian period, which ended around the year1965. It is within the period 1960-1970 that we begin to hear about the normalization of homosexuality, the deconstruction of sexuality, transsexuality, trans-genderism and gender reassignment.[19]

Smith believes that the New Testament supports such a Christian millennium, as that seems to be expressed in Paul's letter to the Galatians when he writes,

There is neither Jew nor Greek, slave nor free, male nor female, for you are all one in Christ, that we might be justified by faith If you belong to Christ, then you are Abraham' seed, and heirs according to the promise. (Gal. 3:28-29).

Such a unity of Jews and Gentiles has been expressed a bit earlier in the Bible, the book of Acts, Chapter 10, where we read the following words,

While Peter was still speaking these words, the Holy Spirit came on all who heard the message. The circumcised believers who had come with Peter were astonished that the gift of the Holy Spirit had been poured out even on the Gentiles. For they heard them speaking in and praising God. (Acts 10:44-46).

Smith has also the following two Bible quotations,

A man is not a Jew if he is only one outwardly, nor is circumcision merely outward and physical. No, man is a Jew if he is one

---

[19] Jonathan Cahn, "*The Return of the Gods,*" Tyndale House Publishers, Inc., Wheaton, II, 60189, 132-138.

inwardly; and circumcision is circumcision of the heart, by the Spirit, not by the written code. Such a man's praise is not from man, but from God. (Ro. 2:28-29).

For it is we who are the circumcision, we who worship by the Spirit of God, who glory in Christ Jesus, and who put no confidence in the flesh. (Phil. 3:3).

The Third Temple

We cannot leave the matter of Israel without making a brief reference to the Jewish expectation of a future Third Temple in Jerusalem. That future Temple is to replace the Second Temple that was destroyed during the earlier mentioned period of AD70. The very first Temple, so-called Solomon's Temple, was destroyed during the Babylonian siege of Jerusalem in 587 BC. The desire for longing to have the Third Temple seem to be the most sacred place of worship for Jews, and especially within Orthodox Judaism. (more on p. 217)

For a biblical reference to the slaughter of a red heifer, needed before using the Temple, is found in the book of Numbers, Chapter 19,

1 The LORD said to Moses and Aaron: 2 "This is the requirement of the law that the LORD has commanded: 'Tell the Israelites to bring you a red heifer without defect or blemish and that has never been under a yoke. 3 Give it to Eleazar the priest; it is to be taken outside the camp and slaughtered in his presence. 4 The Eleazar the priest is to take some of its blood on his finger and sprinkle it seven times toward the front of the Tent of Meeting. (Nu.19:1-3).

Note: The red heifer is needed, as it is the key to make the Temple work like it is supposed to be.

Various voices on the future reality of a Third temple in Jerusalem are of the opinion that this Third Temple will be built in the future. However, it is almost certain, that the building of a future Third Temple will most certainly be contested by Muslims within and throughout the

Middle East, thereby not forgetting the existence of the Dome of the Rock. While there are already tensions between Jews and Muslims over the so called Temple Mount, including the latest trouble with Hamas, it seems that, according to informed opinions, most of the international community has, so far, refrained from recognizing any sovereignty over Jerusalem due to conflicting territorial claims between Israel and the Palestinian National Authority.[20]

Apostle Paul, speaking of the Man of Lawlessness, identified as the coming Antichrist, *a man doomed to destruction* (vs. 3) wrote that,

> 4 He will oppose and will exalt himself over everything that is called God or is worshiped, so that he sets himself up in God's temple, proclaiming himself to be God. (2 Thess. 2:4).

As that future moment will become a reality at some point in time, Christians may look beyond that terrible time, which will come with the coming of the Antichrist, and so will be the coming, lasting reality of a temple as revealed in Revelation 21, being the Church or the Bride of Jesus Christ. That being the case, we may wonder how this future Antichrist can take his place in a possible future Third Temple understood as the future, ultimate Church.

P.S. More on the Third Temple, see p. 217. For now, we may wonder how Christians will be challenged in their faith and their personal relationship to Jesus Christ, as that will be severely tested in these and coming days about sexual immorality. One thing is certain, once faith in and relationship with Christ will continue to be tested, it will bring us to our knees to pray for spiritual strength and perseverance for our children, grandchildren and future generations of Christians.

Jonathan Cahn, in his book, *The Return of the gods* (2022) writes, as mentioned earlier, that

> A pre-Christian nation may erect an altar of human sacrifice. But a post-Christian nation will build Auschwitz.

---

[20] Wikipedia article "Status of Jerusalem."

What Cahn refers to is the murdering of 6 million Jews in concentrations camps during WW II in Poland (Auschwitz) and Germany by the Germans. That gruesome murdering of Jews happened about twenty years before the end of the so-called Christian period. Cahn predicts that the murdering of Jews will continue during the post-Christian period beginning around the middle of 1960s. That is a very serious prediction for the well-being of and peace for the Jewish people now and into the future. However, his prediction had already turned into reality, as we have already learned on October 7, 2024.

There are many cases of persecution of Jews these days, not the least in Israel itself. One example of persecution of Jews just came in on June 2, 2023, via The Epoch Times. The following information came from Jeffrey A. Tucker entitled: "How Jews were Scapegoated During the Pandemic,"

> It was common in the Middle Ages for Jews to get the blame for the spreading of disease. In the 14th century, Jews were accused of poisoning wells, infecting the water with something terrible that was then transferred to the whole community. Scapegoating Jews is a habit with ancient origins. It is an ominous sign and a terrible omen of what is to follow. Indeed, the treatment of the Jews in any society is a "canary in a coal mine.
>
> When they are unjustly blamed for social ills, nothing good follows. We know this from all experiences dating to the ancient world. As a precondition of the attack, please recall that governments all over the country forbid in-person community religious worship. They shut down churches, chapels, synagogues, temples, everything, all in the name of disease control.

Moshe Krakowski of the Tablet has finally documented the outrage of scapegoating Jews (in New York). He points out,

> In April of 2020, [Bill] de Blasio issued a special 'message to the Jewish community' threatening that 'the time for warnings

has passed' and indicated that he would be dispatching the police to 'arrest those who gather in large groups.' Jews were the only ones among the city's many ethnic groups whom de Blasio singled out for public condemnation…And yet a few months later, the mayor was defending BLM protestors and their right to gather.

Brief Overview of some Old-Testament Bible verses re Israel's Future[21]

1. Deuteronomy 28:63-66 speaks of Israel's persecution, holocaust and her rebirth.

Isaiah 42:5-6; Is. 49:6 speaks of Israel being a light to the nations.

Isaiah 60:1-4 speaks of hope (Israel to be a light to the world); 60:15, 18, 19.

Isaiah 61: 1-2: Is. 61:4-6 speak of the Messiah and His days / Is. 61:7.

Isaiah 62: 1-4 The Lord's delight in you…be married.

Isaiah 62:6-7 The Lord's wonderful promises.

Romans 11: All Israel will be saved, (God's favored nation).

2. Israelites being driven out into exile: 586 B.C.

Ezekiel 36 and 37.

Ezekiel saw a restored Israel (dry bones in Israel Ez. 37) physical return of Israel.

3. Jeremiah 31:30-34: (Unconditional covenant) Israel back in the Middle East in 1948.

4. Picture ending Holocaust - Happened in 1948!

---

[21] John Tweedie's "The Prophetic Connection;" Tweedie's Book: "Revelation." www.c4i.ca

CHAPTER THREE
SEXUAL IMMORALITY

As an opening remark, we may readily agree that the subject of sexual immorality is a rather sensitive issue, certainly within Christianity. It is Jesus Christ Himself who addresses this matter in both Old and New Testaments as we learn from the overview of Bible texts mentioned in Appendix A. We will spend some time discussing this potent and rather dominating issue in this Chapter Three, as it is a reality within many Christian families, including our own family. This discussion is meant to help us realize that involvement in such a lifestyle is more hurting than helping people living healthy lives.

THREE PUBLICATIONS on IMMORALTY

From: HiWRITERS on MORALITY IN THE CHURCH AND ITS EFFECTS ON CHURCH GROWTH
There is concern about the rate the subject of immorality is making waves in society; morality is on its decline and in decay. There is gross retrogression on moral ethics in the modern society. The Church, as a religious institution, is to set up examples of moral standards in society, while not being exempted from the claws and threat of immorality ravaging the modern world.

It is recommended that the Church provides basic training on disciplinary standards for her members. This could include the use of internet, bible literatures, audio and visuals aids, and to be skillful in modern technology. The researcher also recommended that the Church also needs to educate their members about various forms of immorality and its consequences and thereby teaching them Gods standard of holiness.

From: EDUPROJECT.COM.NG
Morality today…is increasingly on the decay. Ethics, as a way of ordered living that propagates ideal communal life, and human relationship, is rapidly waning. There is also concern about the rate immorality is making waves in the society; the likely outcome is that there might be a serious breakdown of law and order which could lead to anarchy. It is said that a lawless and immoral society is prone to chaotic situations and anarchy.

From: Jonathan Cahn's book, '*The RETURN of the GODS*'
This book describes the subject of sexual immorality in various ways on different occasions. Regarding the Occult Revival, Cahn writes,

> The same decade that witnessed America's turning from God, the beginning of the sexual revolution, the overturning of gender, the weakening of the family, and the dissemination of mind-altering substances also witnessed a massive revival in the occult. The spiritual void left in God's absence drew millions into a dark spirituality. p. 90.

The context in which Jonathan Cahn wrote these and similar observations about the sexual revolution was the transformation of American culture during the 1960s. He thereby referred to an article in LIFE magazine (1960) describing the following three elements: 'sex, drugs and rock,' or sexuality, intoxicating substances and music. My reason for drawing attention to this information is to indicate that the issue of sexual immorality is part of a dramatic change in the North American culture since the 1960s.

My personal observation is that the subject of sexual immorality has started more recently to impact North America, following the example of Western Europe during the 1980's and 1990's. Jonathan Cahn explains that the phenomenon of sexual immorality is also impacting churches all over the North- American continent. This has already been the case quite some time ago in Europe, certainly in the Western part of the Netherlands, where my wife Louisa and I grew up. The impact of sexual immorality has not only impacted e.g. the Dutch society, but also has led to the closing of numerous church doors, including both our local churches we grew up in. We are now experiencing this sad trend on the North-American continent starting more than decade ago.

Discussion on Sexual Immorality

We may listen to what the following two persons have been saying about sexual immorality, namely Brittany Rust and Rob Wuethrich. Brittany Rustm.[22]

Sexual immorality is certainly not beneficial. Brittany Rust says,

Paul continues in verse 18 of 1 Cor. 6, declaring that, while all other sins are outside the body, sexual immorality is an act of sin against the body, as the body is a temple to the Holy Spirit. This is a vital warning to the dangers of sexual sin and its effects on a person, not just physically and emotionally, but also spiritually. What do we do with this knowledge regarding the dangers of sexual immorality? We do well to take seriously the words found in verse 18, "flee." Run in the opposite direction of the temptation and scenarios that lead to such sin.

In my (Peter) years of pastoral ministry, I've heard the question, "How far can I go before sexual behaviour is technically a sin?" My personal advice is to never ask yourself that question—it's a dangerous mindset that plays with sin. I've always encouraged others to ask what the boundary is, and how far you can stay away from it. You see, a true and firm believer in Christ will not at all, or not easily, flirt with temptation. He or she should never give Satan any foothold. In fact, stay far from the path of destruction. God reminds us that in every temptation, there is a way out.

Brittany Rust's additional comment,

---

22 Brittany Rust, a contributing writer, explains sexual immorality from a biblical perspective under the heading: 'What the Bible says About Sexual Immorality.' She is the founder of Truth and Grace Ministries, Truth x Grace Women, and is the author of five books. Learn more at www.brittanyrust.com.

The Bible passage of 1 Corinthians 10:13 is used by Paul to encourage Christians to keep their focus on God, so they don't stumble and fall. But even if they do, God is gracious enough to provide a way out, which will always involve turning back to Him. Grace is available to us, even on the other side of sin. When we reflect on true repentance, mercy is extended. But again, that goes back to 1 Corinthians 6:12 that just because grace is available to you isn't an endorsement to do what you'd like.

Warning Signs and Avoidance of Sexual Immorality

What are those warning signs to keep an eye out for? First, remember that when you start asking the question of how close you can get, is a warning sign by itself. It's a temptation that knocks at the door. Another warning sign is the moment you find yourself making compromises, like a car ride with a married co-worker here, a little flirting there. Or watching questionable shows or movies with nudity. Another warning sign is that inner morality light that goes off when you're flirting with temptation. Those temptations and the flirting with boundary lines can send a wave of excitement and temptation.

One can avoid sexual immoral behavior by identifying and/or acknowledge his or her weaknesses so that you can take the next step—establish boundaries, as well as implementing guardrails in your life. For example, refuse to be alone in a space with the person you are dating. Also, get the app on your phone and computer that blocks porn and nudity. Again, hold the boundary line!

Remind yourself that human beings are very good at blurring the lines when they want to. I've done it, Rust acknowledges, it was by blurring the lines and not holding the boundaries my boyfriend and I had established that led to sex outside of marriage.

Rob Wuethrich, in his '*Warning Against Sexual Immorality*,' (10/19/2020), sees himself as 'a watchmen, warning people against sexual immorality,' wonders why 'the vast majority of pastors do not want to preach." As a retired pastor, I (Peter) think he could be right in holding such an opinion. In answering his own question Wuethrich says,

The reason why he thinks that he says 'probably because, as a pastor, you must define sexual immorality. And when you do, there will be people who will take offense at the definition.' As a retired pastor, I may add that another reason for such silence is that the pastor concerned is of the opinion that homosexual relationships are OK.

Wuethrich continues by saying that sexual immorality is a huge problem all around us. Then he also says that, biblically speaking,

Sexual immorality is defined as any activity, (in the realm of sexuality), that lies outside a marriage relationship, and that, biblically speaking, a marriage relationship is defined as one man and one woman. Sexual immorality would therefore include such activities as having sexual relations before you're married. It includes having sexual relations with someone who is not your marriage partner, as well as having sexual relations with someone of the same sex.

Commenting on Jesus' Sermon on the Mount, he says,

I tell you that anyone who looks at a woman lustfully has already committed adultery with her in his heart (Matt. 5:28).

Wuethrich further explains,

Jesus is here referring to the sin of "lust," not the sin of "sexual immorality." Furthermore, Jesus was not saying that if you look at a woman lustfully you've committed actual "physical" adultery with her.

Pornography is also a sexual sin, but falls under "lust," while having sexual relations with anything outside our species is defined biblically as sodomy. He thereby explains that in the Bible sodomy is also the term used on several occasions, thereby referring to homosexuality.

On the Internet we also find out that sexual immorality plays a major role in our society…if Christians don't warn people of the dangers of sexual immorality, no one else will. There are sufficient reasons why we, Christians, need to sound the alarm of warning when it comes to sexual immorality.

Passages like Ezekiel 18:20, Romans 6:23, and James 1:15 speak of sin and its consequences. Sexual immorality, like any other sin, separates us from our Creator and ultimately leads to death. As Christians, we need to act as watchmen and warn our friends and family of the pain, suffering, and ultimately, the spiritual death that accompanies sexual misconduct. If we don't do it, the culture in which we live certainly won't.

Note: Following the above discussion on sexual immorality, the reader is strongly encouraged to read APPENDIX A to learn what the Bible says about sexual immorality in the Old and New Testaments, including warnings from Jesus.

Wuethrich also reminds us of what Dr. Ken Scheneck, associate professor of biblical studies at Indiana Wesleyan University, wrote,

Paul has already warned the Corinthians that sexual sin has a corrupting effect on the church, the "body" of Christ. This is the kind of yeast that works its way through the whole lump. Then we may listen to the following insight, namely 'that we were designed to be in a monogamous relationship with one person … one man and one woman in a life-long relationship through the covenant of marriage. The act of sexual intimacy has a way of binding two people into that "one flesh" as the Bible calls it … relationally, physically, emotionally, mentally, as well as spiritually…Therefore, sexual experiences, apart from marriage, create intimate bonds within illegitimate relationships. Sexual intimacy is too powerful to be wielding incorrectly.

We were made for intimacy…intimacy with God, and quite possibly, an earthly example of that relationship with a marital spouse. Sexual immorality messes with that intimacy, destroying the person in the process...We need to not only warn the world we live in, but folks in the church as well.... remember Paul was writing all this to members of the Corinthian church...We need to share the truth with them ... the "truth in love...but the truth, nonetheless. That's what watchmen do.... and now, more than ever, we need watchmen who warn our world of the dangers of sexual immorality.

Following is a series of personal written concerns regarding the acceptance of sexual immoral relationships within my own church community during recent years, and addressed to church council:

IMMORALITY: An Effective Tool in the Hands of Satan

It's sad to hear voices in church communities state that the Bible allows them to invite and embrace those who live in homosexual relationships. They state their opinion to purportedly help listeners understand a particular text according to their human-inspired insights. In so doing, they also try to convince themselves of the correctness of their conceived insights.

At this point, we need to remember that Jesus was personally involved in the creation of the first man and woman, Adam and Eve. Though both people were created without sin, they were listening to and acting upon Satan's convincing but manipulative words that first Eve, and through Eve also Adam, ate from the fruit which was strictly forbidden by God (Genesis 3). Like that creation story and Man's Fall, we see how Christ's serious warning not to participate in an immoral lifestyle is now overruled by sinful man's reasoning that such lifestyle is OK.

At this point, we need to listen to what the Lord Jesus Christ said in His closing words in the last book of the Bible, Rev. 22,

> Behold, I am coming soon! My reward is with me, and I will give to everyone according to what he has done. I am Alpha and the Omega, the First and the Last, the Beginning and the End. Blessed are those who wash their robes, that they may have the right to the tree of life and may go through the gates into

the city. Outside are the dogs, those who practice magic arts, the sexually immoral, the murderers, the idolaters and everyone who loves and practices falsehood. (Rev. 22:14-15).

Denying or ignoring the above-written warning of Jesus in Revelation 22, as well as similar warnings in the Bible that ignore the Holy Spirit, our present Counselor (John 14:16, 26). We also could speak of being influenced by sinful human nature and thus against Jesus' will.

There is a story in the Bible in which Satan felt that he had the ability to have Jesus taking his ideas serious. We find such occasion in Matthew 4:1-10, when Jesus came back from his 40-day stay in the wilderness, being extremely tired. On that occasion, Jesus, while dealing with extreme physical exhaustion, did not submit Himself to Satan's manipulative directives, as He simply appealed to the Bible to which Satan had no response, and disappeared.

Considering that historic event mentioned in above paragraphs, we need to ask ourselves what really leads some Christians embrace immoral lifestyles. What motivates and convinces them to openly support those living one of various immoral lifestyles? To find another biblical answer to that important question, we may turn to Paul's second letter to the Corinthians, chapter 11. Here we find the answer to the above question,

> ...I am afraid that just as Eve was deceived by the serpent's cunning, your minds may somehow be led astray from your sincere and pure devotion to Christ. (2 Cor. 11:3).

Following the above-stated words of Paul, we may also listen to the following Bible verses,

> As surely as the truth of Christ is in me, nobody in the regions of Achaia will stop this boasting of mine. Why? Because I do not love you? God knows I do! And I will keep on doing what I am doing to cut the ground from under those who want an opportunity to be considered equal to us in the things they boast about. For such men are false apostles, deceitful

workmen, masquerading as apostles of Christ. And no wonder, for Satan himself masquerades as an angel of light. It is not surprising, then, if his servants masquerade as servants of righteousness. Their end will be what their actions deserve. (2 Cor. 11:10-15).

With those Spirit-inspired words of Paul, we may have found the main cause of the problems we are facing in our churches today concerning the issue of immorality. Satan is extremely clever in successfully manipulating Christians to become disobedient to Jesus' clear instructions regarding immorality. Satan knows the weaknesses of sinful people, including Christians, and how to play them by making those people following him, and leading him, Satan, say 'yes!'

These days, many Christians believe in Jesus, while unaware of their own spiritual weaknesses. One such weakness is listening to and, without realizing, fall for Satan's manipulative influence that living the homosexual lifestyle is OK. Thus, we find in various churches people who, without hesitation, agree with, and maybe even indulge themselves in one of various immoral lifestyles.

Allowing Satan's influence direct one's thinking and behavior is, in and by itself, a sign of betraying the truth of God's Word, and thus Jesus, who is the Truth. Thereby comes a lack of attention for another important part of God's Word, namely the aspect of 'healing.' In all what proponents of immoral lifestyles say or write, one does not hear about this one central theme in the Bible: the need for spiritual, as well as physical healing. This lack of understanding is also a clear sign that something is seriously amiss in all the rhetoric and attitudes of those sympathetic to the homosexual lifestyle.

When we hear from those who think very positively about the homosexual lifestyle, thereby using terms such as love, respect and acceptance, and maintaining peace, we may think of different kinds of love, respect, acceptance and peace. As Christian, we need to place these terms in light of the first and greatest biblical commandment that teaches that we need to show <u>all</u> our love, respect, acceptance and peace for and towards the Lord our God. Only then we know how to show and direct proper love, respect acceptance and peace to our neighbors.

What Christians need to realize is that Satan is not only strongly motivated but also is able to single out Christians who are quite sensitive to worldly opinions about immoral behavior that could have negative consequences. This is often true when it is realized that one raises objections against immoral behavior. This is true not only at work, but also true in schools, churches and families.

To avoid any negative reaction or opinion about one's opposition to sexual immoral behavior, one may decide not to share his or her controversial opinion with others. The consequence of sharing one's honest opinion that sexual immoral lifestyle is inappropriate could lead to being ostracized. That can happen, and it is happening at school, at work and even at church. I know.

Christians today are facing a serious dilemma when it comes to agreeing or disagreeing with what the Bible says regarding immoral behavior. Certainly, as Christians, we have also come to the point of making a firm choice: keeping life as simple as possible by agreeing with any of the immoral lifestyles or making a stand for Jesus by taking the consequences of disagreeing with such lifestyles. Such a firm stand can be taken based on the following Bible text: "*For we cannot do anything against the truth, but only for the truth.*" 2 Cor. 13:8.

Considering the last paragraph concerning Christians facing and dealing with sexual immoral lifestyles, we may listen to what our brother in Christ, Lucas Miles, wrote about Christians dealing with so-called Trojan horses, under the heading: Theological Warfare.

Theological Warfare,

Miles informs us that slipping past the walls of Christian orthodoxy and sound doctrine, a barrage of intellectual and spiritual attacks has produced what is now being called "the Christian left"—a growing constituency of "Christians" who have adopted (either knowingly or unknowingly) leftist, socialistic thinking, ideals, values, and innovations.

In the past, those cloak-and-dagger doctrinal deconstruction-ists only existed in select intellectual circles, or within liberal universities. But now it seems the that the 'Trojan horses of the Christian Left' have been activated and even placed on display by mainline Christian institutions, faith-oriented content-cre-ators, and even some local churches—in many cases without their knowledge.[23]

It seems that being more influenced by those belonging to, what s Miles understands as, the Christian left, than by Jesus Christ, is a no-tion I (Peter) agree with. The underlining message from Jesus is found in Bible verses such as 2 Cor. 11:3;10-15; Rev. 2:14-15; Rev. 22: 14, as well as expressed in other parts of God's Word, also including Rom. 1:26-27.

Further readings:

1. My self-published book, *THE RAINBOW LETTERS: Immorali-ty: The Church's Achilles' heel in the Twentieth Century.* Note: My author's name: Rev. Peter Hendriks Okello.

2. The book entitled, *LET JESUS HEAL YOUR HIDDEN WOUNDS: Cooperating with the Holy Spirit in Healing Ministry.* Au-thors: Brad Long & Cindy Strickler.

Jesus on Immoral Behavior

In Matthew 17, we read how Jesus, initially accompanied by Peter, James and John, spoke with Moses and Elijah, while being transfigured. We also read that, at that time apostle Peter spoke to Jesus, a bright cloud enveloped them, and a voice from the cloud said,

This is my Son, whom I love; with Him I am well pleased. Lis-ten to Him! (Matt. 17:5).

Remember, that same heavenly voice continues to speak to all of us who are following and obeying Jesus!

---

[23] Lucas Miles, *THE CHRISTAN LEFT: How liberal Thought has Hijacked the Church*, Broadstreet Publishing Group, LLC, Savage, Minnesota, USA, 2021

It is most important for us to also listen to Jesus, when He speaks to us as well. Therefore, we need to do what Jesus said to those three challenges of Satan in Matthew 4:1-10. In this Bible passage the devil spoke to Jesus by saying, "*If you are the Son of God...*" Now, read verses 3, 6, 9, and take note of the words Jesus said in His responses to Satan's three challenges, beginning with the words, "*It is written...*"

In all three responses Jesus was consistently referring to God's Word, the Bible, respectively Deut. 8:3, Deut. 6:16 and Deut. 6:13,

Deut. 8:3, "He (God) humbled you, causing you to hunger...to

Teach you that man does not live on bread alone but on every word that comes from the mouth of the LORD."

Deut. 6:16, "Do not test the LORD your God..."

Deut. 6:13, "Fear the LORD your God, serve Him only..."

Considering what is written above, we, as followers of Jesus, also need to listen to God the Father and to God the Son, and respond accordingly to Jesus' responses to Satan. When we are dealing with serious issues such as immoral behavior, we also need to listen to what Jesus would say in response, as He has also something urgently to say to us about similar behavior. Listen to what He said to the Church in Pergamum and in Thyatira:

To the Church in Pergamum,

Nevertheless, I have a few things against you. You have people there who hold to the teaching of Balaam, who taught Balak to entice the Israelites to sin by eating food sacrificed to idols and by committing sexual immorality...Repent therefore!" (Rev. 2:14, 16a).

To the Church in Thyatira,

Nevertheless, I have this against you: You tolerate that woman Jezebel, who calls herself a prophetess. By her teaching she misleads my servants into sexual immorality... Rev. 2:20.

In the last chapter of Revelation, Chapter 22, we read Jesus saying,

Blessed are those who wash their robes, that they may have the right to the tree of life and may go through the gates into the city. Outside are the dogs, those who practice magic arts, the sexually immoral, the murderers, the idolaters, and everyone who loves and practices falsehood. (Rev. 22:15).

Then we also read in Rev. 22,

And if anyone takes words away from this book of prophecy, God will take away from him his share in the tree of life and in the holy city, which are described in this book. (Rev. 22:19).

All these words of Jesus were part of His final farewell to all who would read them. Jesus' words of warning are meant to be heard and to be taken seriously throughout <u>all</u> generations. I emphasize 'all' as there are many people today also make the mistake of ignoring such stern warnings. The question is why would anyone throw Jesus' serious warnings in the wind? In answer, we could pose the question, "Who then are Jesus' *real* disciples in our days?"

We read at different places in the Bible that Jesus described His *real* followers as being 'fishers of men," who "deny themselves and take up their cross," to be "those who lose their lives for Jesus," and "those who follow Jesus as they hear His voice."

Note what of Jesus said about little children in Mark 10,

Let the little children come to Me, and do not hinder them, for the kingdom of God belongs to such as these. I tell you the truth, anyone who will not receive the kingdom of God like a little child will never enter it... (Mk. 10:14b-15).

We understand from Jesus' above answer that His *real* disciples are those who listen to His voice, take them to heart, and then continue to follow Him, no matter what the consequences will or could be. Real followers of Jesus don't dispute, don't misinterpret, don't overlook, nor change the meaning of His words.

Then, take also note of Jesus' following words in Rev. 22,

Blessed are those who wash their robes, that they may have the right to the tree of life…" (Rev. 22:14). John also warns us that, "… if anyone takes words away from this book of prophecy, God will take away from him his share in the tree of life…" (Rev. 22:19a).

As a follow-up to John's above-mentioned warnings, voiced above, we may also listen to Paul's words in his first letter to the Thessalonians, as being inspired by the Holy Spirit,

> …For you know what instructions we gave you by the authority of the Lord Jesus. It is God's will that you should avoid sexual immorality; that each of you should learn to control his own body in a way that is holy and honorable, not in passionate lust like the heathen, who do not know God; and that in this matter no one should wrong his brother or take advantage of him. The Lord will punish men for all such sins, as we have already told you and warned you. For God did not call us to be impure, but to live a holy life. Therefore, he who rejects this instruction does not reject man but God, who gives you his Holy Spirit. (1 Thess. 4:2-8).

The church of the Thessalonians was in an evil, immoral world. Paul understood the influence of that world on that Christian community. He therefore exhorted them to be vigilant, to continue as a witness to Christ, being set apart from that world. He exhorted especially the leaders in the church to be, and to remain, true guardians of the church. In today's world, our church leaders need and should act as true guardians of their churches based on God's Word, the Bible.

However, many Christians, among them church leaders, don't seem to realize the influence of a Satan-driven radical Liberalism (à la Communism, Marxism) in North America. Therefore, Christians do well to compare social realities concerning immoral behavior anywhere in the world with similar realities and biblical warnings against them, as well as how to respond to those realities as staunch followers of Jesus Christ.

Read, for example, NT letters such as Galatians 5; 1 Thess. 4; 2 Thess. 2; Jude, half- brother of Jesus. (Mt. 4:1-11; Eph. 6:10-18).

Turning to Paul's letter to the Galatians, we read in Chapter 5,

> So, I say, live by the Spirit, and you will not gratify the desires of the sinful nature. For the sinful nature desires what is contrary to the Spirit, and the Spirit what is contrary to the sinful nature. They conflict with each other, so that you do not do what you want. But if you are led by the Spirit, you are not under law. The acts of the sinful nature are obvious: sexual immorality... (Gal. 5:16-19a).

Paul on Satanic Influence

In his Roman letter, Paul voices the following warning and encouragement, (next page 81)

> "I urge you, brothers, to watch out for those who cause divisions and put obstacles in your way that are contrary to the teaching you have learned. Keep away from them. For such people are not serving our Lord Christ, but their own appetites. By smooth talk and flattery, they deceive the minds of naïve people. Everyone has heard about your obedience, so I am full of joy over you; but I want you to be wise about what is good, and innocent about what is evil. The God of peace will soon crush Satan under your feet." (Rom. 16:17-20).

In the Book: "*The Christian Left: How Liberal Thought Has Hijacked the Church.*" written by Pastor Lucas Miles, we read words such as '*...* who is 'blowing the whistle...on the Left's nefarious attempt to commandeer the church and to rewrite the foundation of the Christian faith.' Miles also quotes Oliver Thomas, an American Baptist minister regarding the LGBTQ agenda, with the following words,

> It's difficult to watch good people...buy into the sincere but misguided notion that being a faithful Christian means accepting everything the Bible teaches. p.37.

Miles furthermore writes,

'Thomas takes his extra-biblical, Christian-Left ideologies to the hilt by questioning Jesus' capability for knowledge, at the time of His presence on earth, suggesting that the most authoritative biblical figure of all time, Christ Himself, was somehow insufficiently "woke" to the issues of modern society.

According to Thomas, Christ was "limited to what first century humans knew" and, therefore, couldn't possibly be aware of the "million other things the centuries have taught us." (pp.37-38).

Miles' bottom line would be that Christians who ignore Jesus' serious warning neither to listen to and getting involved in, nor approving of immoral lifestyles, are compromising the Lord's headship, as expressed earlier. Therefore, Christians with opposing opinions about the Lord's headship and teachings live in broken fellowship with the Lord and fellow brothers and sisters This is exactly Satan aims for, and very often succeeds in. This reality has developed in the closing of hundreds, if not thousands of church doors in Western Europe during the 1980s and 1990s. Satan is now succeeding in North America as well!

Ignoring Jesus has Serious Consequences
It seems that we are experiencing these days an unraveling of the need to take God's Word as the final word for living in obedience to Him. It seems that living a satisfying and constructive life is no longer to be found in the Bible. As such, the temptation to become free from some Biblical instructions has become for many the way to go.

That Satan is tempting to lead people away from a God-obeying life is one reason that led me (Peter), again to Matthew 4:1-10 in which we hear about Satan tempting Jesus to do his will, and that Jesus' consistent responses to Satan's recurring temptations need to be heeded, most certainly in today's world.

What a precious example we have in Jesus, the Son of God, to know how to respond to imposing challenges by evil forces confronting us today. In Christ we have the lasting example to stand firm according to the words of Jesus spoken to Satan. In those earlier quoted 10 verses in Matthew 4, we have a prime and lasting example, how to respond to those who are being played by Satan, and conveniently accepting those who feel attracted to those of the same sex.

Jesus' First Parable of the Clean and Unclean

In the Gospel of Matthew, especially Matthew 15, we read about Jesus explaining to His disciples, who had asked Him to explain the parable He just had shared with the crowd, namely,

> 10 Listen and understand, 11 What goes into a man's mouth does not make him 'unclean,' but what comes out of his mouth, that is what makes him 'unclean'....15 Peter said, explain the parable to us." 16 "Are you still so dull? Jesus asked them. 17
>
> Don't you see that whatever enters the mouth goes into the stomach and then out of the body? 18 But the things that come out of the mouth come from the heart, and these make a man 'un-clean.' 19 For out of the heart come evil thoughts, murder, adultery, sexual immorality, theft, false testimony, slander.
>
> 20 These are what make a man 'unclean'; but eating with unwashed hands does not make him 'unclean. (Matt. 15:10-11; 15-20).

In the above parable, Jesus makes it very clear that acts of sexual immorality, as well as evil thoughts, murder, adultery, theft, false testimony, slander, are committed by those He calls 'unclean,' and are therefore, subsequently, not accepted by Jesus. 'He who has ears to hear let him hear.'

Following Jesus

Following Jesus is more than believing in Jesus, as it often takes courage to speak up and stand up for Jesus in word and deed, even when it will have inconvenient consequences. As parents, we naturally take actions to protect our children in the face of danger. The same way, followers of Jesus do come into action in face of threats, difficulties, or harmful situations. Such a protective attitude brought Jesus to the cross to open the way to eternal life. It also took the lives of apostles Paul and Peter by speaking up on behalf of Jesus. It took the life of the 39-old German Lutheran pastor and theologian Dietrich Bonhoeffer when he was gruesomely hanged by opposing Nazi policies and their unspeakable atrocities just before WW II had ended in 1945.

Speaking, and/or living, on behalf of Christ, Christians can expect resistance from anti-Christ forces that may lead to inconvenient consequences, even to death. That happened in the past, as it happens today in e.g. China and in Iran through persecution. In present North-American societies, Christians are experiencing a particular kind of persecution called persecution by *word*, and sometimes even by *hurting actions*. This is a persecution by radical Liberals for the purpose of replacing Judeo-Christian values, norms and traditions by radical liberal ideas à la Marxism, Communism.

As Satan is the driving force behind all persecutions, he continues to attack local churches as one of his main goals. He uses hereby immorality, including homosexuality. He knows the spiritual weakness, stamina, of many Christians who may believe in Jesus, but are not following Jesus when faced with uncomfortable situations or circumstances. As such, we may wonder what kind of Jesus they are following.

While believers in Jesus may accept and defend immoral lifestyles, real followers of Jesus may join in standing up for Jesus by rejecting categorically immoral lifestyles within church and society. Such controversies do often lead to schisms in the church. Thereby comes that real and consistent followers of Jesus, may face serious consequences at work: e.g. by being avoided, rejected, even losing one's job and thus much-needed financial income. In such cases, followers of Jesus need to stand together in support of those who may become victimized by standing up for Jesus.

Possible Future

Presently, we have in Canada a new developing situation, in which followers of Jesus could expect serious consequences in their opposition to and rejection of immoral lifestyles. An email received on December 17, 2021, states: 'It is now a crime for pastors to help LGBT people to deal with/overcome non-heterosexual behaviour,' as it has been passed in the House and Senate with unanimous and royal consent.

Considering the various developments within the church, as well as between state and church, we may begin to visualize a situation in which we could have two different churches: one church accepted by the state (Liberal church), and one church rejected by the state (Conservative church). Could we really go down to a society in which we have a state church and an 'underground' church à la China and Iran? Is this a thought worthy of contemplation? Well, the truth is that the church in China and Iran are fast-growing churches! They are churches very blessed by Jesus Christ.

What Jesus do You Believe in?

Some important questions readers may need to answer for themselves is the question what kind of Jesus they want to listen to, follow and obey. It seems helpful that they need to realize how important it is to really know Jesus.

In that case, it seems helpful to turn, for example, to Paul's letter to the Colossians, Chapter 1, that speaks of the Supremacy of Christ,

15 He is the image of the invisible God, the firstborn over all creation. 16 For by Him all things were created: things in heaven and on earth, visible and invisible, whether thrones or powers or rulers or authorities; all things were created by Him and for Him. 17 He is before all things, and in Him all things hold together. 18 And He is the head of the body, the church; He is the beginning and the firstborn from among the dead, so that in everything He might have the supremacy. 19 For God was pleased to have all His fullness dwell in Him, 20 and through Him to reconcile to Himself all things, whether things on earth or things in heaven, by making peace through His blood, shed on the cross. (Col. 1:15-20).

After reading this very significant description of the Lord Jesus Christ, one may realize how small, insignificant and vulnerable each one of us really is. In that light, we may raise serious questions such as, "What Jesus do you think of, speak of, or worship? Is it a Jesus you can simply ignore, and/or set briefly aside as Lord and Savior?"

Those kinds of questions could lead to other questions such as, "What Jesus is used in sermons, in church life, in one's day-to-day life. Is He someone you can easily avoid, not to be taken seriously, or is your Lord at all times, and Who you follow and stand up for, no matter the consequences?"

Concerning the Celebration of the Lord's Supper

Presently, we have many churches with members who are either in favor of, or against sexual immoral lifestyles, and may be involved in sexual immoral relationships. If so, then there are two different groups of Christians in church life and worship: one group that embraces Christ wholeheartedly, the other group denying Jesus, either knowingly or unknowingly. It will be a travesty when these two different groups of Christians come together for the celebration of the Lord's Supper, thereby showing unity in Christ, while in reality there is no unity in Christ.

No blessing will come forth from such a public celebration, on the contrary, such a demonstration of disunity is an absolute disgrace to Jesus. It is a serious affront to unity, though pretending blessings upon such a demonstration of disregard for real unity in Christ.

Please take note of the Heidelberg Catechism, Q/A 81:

81 Q. Who are to come to the Lord's Table?[24]

A. Hypocrites and those who are unrepentant…eat and drink judgment on themselves?

The basis of that answer is found in 1 Cor. 11,

27 Therefore, whoever eats the bread or drinks the cup of the Lord in an unworthy manner will be guilty of sinning against the

[24] PSALTER HYMNAL, CRC Publications, Grand Rapids1989.

body and blood of the Lord. 28 A man ought to examine himself before he eats of the bread and drinks of the cup. 29 For anyone who eats and drinks without recognizing the body of the Lord eats and drinks judgment on himself. (1 Cor. 11:27-29).

One conclusion that can be drawn from the above Bible passage of 1 Cor. 11:27-29 is that not only one or more church members could be involved in a sexual immoral relationship, but also members who agree that such a relationship is allowed. If that is the case, we need to remind ourselves that, based on God's Word, the Bible, that they could well be recipients of God's displeasure.

One can see that in case the pastor, council members and church members are all OK with sexual immoral relationship that they thereby need to realize that, eventually, God will respond the way He sees fit. It could, indeed, lead to the closing of church doors.

Another, unrelated problem is that some Christians may have to face and deal with the possibility that one's own child, or grand-child, is attractive to or even live already in a same-sex relationship. Then also, another person may raise the problem of having difficulties at work when colleagues or boss realize that he or she is against homosexual relationships. Such a situation at work could be easily avoided by just joining those who welcome such unbiblical ways of living.

It does not hurt to be reminded of the last words of Jesus found in Rev. 22,

Blessed are those who wash their robes, that they may have the right to the tree of life…" (Rev. 22:14). John, inspired by the Holy Spirit, warns us that, "… if anyone takes words away from this book of prophecy, God will take away from him his share in the tree of life… (Rev. 22:19a).

Realizing who Jesus is, as previously described in Col. 1:15-20 (see above, p. 85), one may come to realize how small and insignificant each one of us really is. We may thereby also realize that ignoring Jesus' warnings concerning immoral behavior could lead to serious consequences.

Please read Rev. 2:14-16a and Rev. 22: 14-15, as mentioned earlier. In addition, we may say that this matter of sexual immorality is already creating great tension in many Christian families.

We may agree with the fact that, especially among the younger generations, we see an increase in sexual immoral behavior, both within and outside Christian families. It seems also true that, for the sake of peace in the family, some parents choose not to confront or oppose their children who are involved in such lifestyles. If that is the case, one could ask those parents what is more important: Keeping peace within their families, or having and keeping peace with Jesus who, we know, is firmly against immoral lifestyles.

Considering the above paragraph, the following rather painful words of Jesus, mentioned in Matthew 10, need to draw special attention,

> 34 *Do not suppose that I have come to bring peace to the earth. I did not come to bring peace, but the sword. 35 For I have come to turn 36 'a man against his father, a daughter against her mother, a daughter-in-law against her mother-in-law—36 a man's enemies will be the members of his own household.* (Matt. 10:34-36).

Then also listen to the following words of Jesus in the next Bible passage,

> 37 *Anyone who loves his father or mother more than Me is not worthy of Me; anyone who loves his son or daughter more than Me is not worthy of Me; 38 and anyone who does not take his cross and follow Me is not worthy of Me. 39 Whoever finds his life will lose it, and whoever loses his life for My sake will find it.* Matt. 10:37-39. Read also Luke 9:23-26.

One Last Question

One needs to answer the following two-part question:

What Jesus do you believe in and worship:

 a. A Jesus you believe in and worship no matter what the consequences will be, or

b. A Jesus you can ignore when it comes to immorality, or for any other reason.

Remember that Jesus has expressed very clearly His opinion on such lifestyles!

Note: one answer leads to salvation, the other answer could well keep your salvation at bay. Reformer John Huss reminds us of the following Bible text,

> For we cannot do anything against the truth, but only for the truth. (Cor.13:8).

Also note: In APPENDIX A we find a series of many OT and NT Bible passages concerning sexual immorality, written by Holy Spirit-inspired persons, and by Jesus Himself, all who have voiced their stern warning not to get involved in sexual immoral lifestyles.

Apostle Paul wrote,

> 11 But now am writing you that you must not associate with anyone who calls himself a brother but is sexually immoral or greedy, an idolator or a slanderer, a drunkard or a swindler. With such a man do not even eat. (1 Cor. 5:11).

Paul also wrote about living by the Spirit in the following words in Galatians 5,

> 16 So I say, live by the Spirit, and you will not gratify the desires of the sinful nature…19 The acts of sinful nature are obvious: sexual immorality…21 I warn you, as I did before, that those who live like this will not inherit the kingdom of God. (Gal. 5:16, 19, 21).

Paul's words of warning in Galatians 5 are to be taken seriously.

IMMORALITY: THREE KINDS OF FAITH

Steadfast, Unwavering Faith

We may turn to the end of the book of Revelation, Chapter 22, where we read the following words of Jesus:

> 12 Behold I am coming soon! My reward is with me, and I will give to everyone according to what he has done. 13 I am the Alpha and the Omega, the First and the Last, the Beginning and the End. 14 "Blessed are those who wash their robes, that they may have the right to the tree of life and may go through the gates into the city. 15 Outside are the dogs, those who practice magic arts, the sexual immoral, the murderers, the idolaters, and everyone who loves and practices falsehood. (Rev. 22:12-15).

Vulnerable Faith

On November 6, 2022, my wife Louisa and I listened to Rabbi Schneider (a Messianic Jew) teaching on the Bible passage: Rom. 16:17-20. The apostle Paul wrote in these verses:

> 17 I urge you, brothers, to watch out for those who cause divisions and put obstacles in your way that are contrary to the teaching you have learned. **Keep away from them**. 18 For such people are not serving our Lord Christ, but their own appetites. By smooth talk and flattery, they deceive the minds of naïve people. 19 Everyone has heard about your obedience, so I am full of joy over you; but I want you to be wise about what is good, and innocent about what is evil. The God of peace will soon crush Satan under your feet. Rom. 16:17-20.

Rabbi Schneider, a serious Bible teacher, gave a helpful exposition of the above Bible passage. It is one of numerous Bible passages not taken into consideration by those who continue to defy that homosexual behavior is not approved of in God's Word, including Revelation 2 and 22, quoted earlier. As a matter of fact, they accept and defend such behavior as being acceptable in our time and age.

Considering a Bible passage such as Rom. 16:17-20, we need to urge one another to take such Bible passage most seriously, as we should do with all of Scripture. Among his explanations of these Bible verses, this rabbi warns us not to doubt God's authority, as such an attitude invites Satan, who has only one thing in mind, namely, to turn us away from God's Word. As a result, those Christians will not be able to serve the Lord according to His will. On the contrary, this Bible teacher warns Christians not to doubt God's Word, but instead to accept it, and to stand up for His Word with its lasting authority, as it provides us with the power to successfully resist Satan and his temptations.

In my earlier mentioned book, *THE RAINBOW LETTERS: IMMORALITY: THE CHURCH'S ACHILLES HEEL*, I mention several reasons for accepting immoral behavior, among them fear and anxiety for the consequences of opposing growing public acceptance of such behavior. We are presently dealing with the reality that the Bible passage of Rom. 16:17-20 explains clearly to remain obedient to what God wants us to do when Bible-opposing and ignoring voices are giving un-acceptable direction to church communities. As can be expected, many Christians are sensitive to opposing voices from the world around them.

Healing Faith

It is obvious that one's feelings could be stronger than one's faith, especially on an issue such as immoral behavior. Is it not true that through determined, unwavering faith in the truth of God's authoritative Word, we have the strength to oppose successfully Satan's corrupt manipulations through the guidance of the Holy Spirit.

It is important to realize that in all our deliberations on immoral behavior issues God's authority needs to raise above human feelings of fear and anxiety. This needs to be ready, personally and as a local church, to deal with a possible backlash, that could include financial loss. However, we should not forget that, as a church, or as an individual, we need to demonstrate a steadfast, unwavering faith, that includes *healing* faith.

It is through *healing* faith that a local church, and therefore each individual member, can help and support people to overcome appreciation for and involvement with immoral behavior. It is through strong and prayer-filled faith and fellowship with brothers and sisters in the Lord, that we can stop and drive out Satan's influence in someone's life, and so in any local church. Such communal faith and prayer help us to bring about healing, restoration and a positive witness to the restoring and encouraging power of the Holy Spirit.

In the meantime, we need to support those believers, who make a stand for Jesus and the biblical truth regarding the wrongness of immoral lifestyles, in any way we can, including financial support. Involvement in a small group could be very helpful in support of those who are dealing with the consequences of standing their ground in obedience to God's Word. How useful a Bible passage, such as Rom. 16:17-20, is in understanding God's will regarding immoral behavior.

In all this, we hear in Rom. 16 the following advice,

I want you to be wise about what is good, and innocent about what is evil. (Rom. 16:20).

In applying such commendation in our daily lives, we can count on God's help and the Spirit's guidance in supporting one another to stand up for Jesus, no matter the consequences.

Note: Again, for an extensive exposition of Bible verses that directly speak to immoral lifestyle(s), please see APPENDIX A.

The Bible Speaks

Having read the above-mentioned references to APPENDIX A with its many Bible verses on immoral behavior, we see the clear message of God's Word that living in a homosexual relationship is wrong, seriously warned for and strongly condemned. It raises the question how many Christians, including spiritual leaders, not only support such unbiblical relationships, but are leading church members away from God's Word.

Such realities make us to ponder the reality of similar developments among Christians in the local churches. So, let us ponder Jesus' three responses to Satan's suggestions to seriously consider his suggestions we read about in Matthew 4:

Jesus' <u>first</u> response:

It is written: Man does not live on bread alone, but on every word that comes from the mouth of God. (Matt. 4:4).

Jesus' <u>second</u> response:

It is also written: Do not put the Lord your God to the test. Matt.: 7:7.

Jesus' <u>third</u> response:

Away from Me, Satan! For it is written: 'Worship the Lord your God and serve Him only. (Matt. 4:10).

The lesson Jesus teaches in Matthew 4:1-10, is an unwavering message to us, which is to be and to remain obedient to the Word of God. We need to follow Jesus' example by standing up against Satan on the bases of God's Word. It is my observation that those in support of living immoral lifestyles are not really interested in God's Word with its strong opinion on living such lifestyles. This is a most critical issue in today's world.

While facing many strong challenges the world throws at us, individual Christians and church communities alike, need to resist Satan in his efforts to destroy them. Yes, Satan is challenging churches to listen to him and thereby drawing many Christians into types of sexual behavior that oppose God's will. Many Christians have already fallen in Satan's trap to live a life free from so called outdated biblical warnings. But then, how outdated is opposition to God?

A Christian Response
Present realities tell us that Satan has significant influence in the world, and most certainly on Christians. We are facing the possibility that a

great percentage of Christians turn a deaf ear to the overwhelming number of warnings in the Bible not to engage in immoral behavior. How come that in many local churches spiritual leadership turns a deaf ear to the many warnings in the Bible not to follow the ways of the world?

What is the real motivation of so many Christians not to be restricted by what the Bible explicitly tells us not to do? What is it that drives Christians to ignore Jesus Christ's serious warning concerning immorality, and follow their own desire to live the way they desire? Again, how come that so many Christian leaders, pastors, council members, don't use the Bible to guide and teach their congregations to remain obedient to Jesus? It seems that we are talking here about a serious lack of Biblical leadership in various churches, and likely in many families?

In all this commotion about immoral lifestyles we need to remember how Jesus stood up for people like us by His suffering prior to His crucifixion, as we read in Matthew 27:

> The governor's soldiers took Jesus into the Praetorium…They stripped Him and put a scarlet robe on Him and then twisted together a crown of thorns and set it on His head. They put a staff in His right hand and knelt in front of Him and mocked Him. "Hail, king of the Jews!" they said. They spit on Him and took the staff and struck Him on the head again and again. (Matt. 27:27-30).

That immense painful and deeply humiliating event during three long hours, Jesus finally cried out in a loud voice, *"Eloi, Eloi, lama sabachthani?"* which means, *"My God, My God, why have You forsaken Me?"* (Matt. 27:46). In a response to that horrible event, in which Jesus gave His life to give us eternal life, we need to ask ourselves this question: How can anyone, any Christian, accept immorality Jesus condemns unequivocally? Let this serious question think in!

Like Jesus endured that most excruciating suffering for mankind's salvation, let us then also stand with Jesus and His Word by listening to and following Him in faith and determination, rather than showing arrogance by ignoring Jesus, who stood up against Satan manipulating suggestions for you and me.

It seems that a vast majority of those living in North America have no knowledge of what has happened in Western Europe some 30-40 years ago. During those years, hundreds of churches per month had to close their doors due to a sharp decline of worshippers. And now, we already hear of the splitting of congregations, and even of denominations, on our North American continent over the issue of immoral behavior.

Please take note that Christianity in Western Europe has seriously diminished. Now, Satan, with so much experience concerning his triumphant work in Western Europe, is trying to accomplish the same thing on the N.A. continent. He will undoubtedly succeed if we, Christians, don't stand up against him by standing up for Jesus, no matter what the consequences are going to be.

After 20 years of working as a mechanical and industrial engineer in both the Netherlands and Canada, before the Lord let me into pastoral ministry, I (Peter) realize fully well that one may find it quite inconvenient, if not difficult, to work in an office, or in a local church, with those who have accepted immoral lifestyles as normal. Christians in most work environments will, or are already do, face inconvenient situations, as they are living up to Jesus' expectations. But then, Jesus also knows about your specific situation at work, as the Holy Spirit will undoubtedly guide you in how to deal with opposing, even belligerent situations. As already mentioned before, local churches need to be ready to assist and support brothers and sisters in the Lord in such situations.

Followers of Jesus in a Divisive World
Not Peace but Division, Luke 12,

> 51 Do you think I (Jesus) came to bring peace on earth? No, I tell you, but division. 52 From now on there will be five in one family divided against each other, three against two and two against three. 53 They will be divided, father against son and son against father, mother against daughter and daughter

against mother, mother-in-law against daughter-in-law, and daughter-in-law against mother-in-law. (Lk. 12:51-53)

Following Jesus Unequivocally, Jn. 14,

23 Jesus replied (to Judas Iscariot), "If anyone loves Me, he will obey My Teaching. My Father will love him, and we will come to him and make Our home with him. 24 He who does not love Me will not obey My teaching. These words you hear are not My own; they belong to the Father who sent me. 25 "All this I have spoken while still with you. 26 But the Counselor, the Holy Spirit, whom the Father will send in My name, will teach you all things and will remind you of everything I have said to you." (Jn. 14:23-26).

More Than Conquerors, Rom. 8,

28 And we know that in all things God works for the good of those who love Him, who have been called according to His purpose. 29 For those God foreknew He also predestined to be conformed to the likeness of His Son, that He might be the firstborn among many brothers. 30 And those He predestined, He also called; those He called, He also justified; those He justified, He also glorified." (Rom. 8:28-30).

The Armor of God, Ephesians 6

10 Finally, be strong in the Lord and in His mighty power. 11 Put on the full armor of God so that you can take your stand against the devil's schemes. 12 For our struggle is not against flesh and blood, but against the rulers, against the authorities, against the powers of this dark world and against the spiritual forces of evil in the heavenly realms. 13 Therefore put on the full armor of God, so that when the day of evil comes, you may

be able to stand your ground, and after you have done everything to stand. 14 Stand firm then... (Eph. 6:10-13) then (Eph.
6:14-18).

Paul speaking to Timothy

12 "In fact, everyone who wants to live a godly life in ChristJe-
sus will be persecuted, (2 Tim. 3:12).

What Paul is saying here, not only to Timothy but to all Christians,
is that standing up for the truth that living in an immoral relationship is
wrong, will have repercussions that will be hurting, could well make life
unpleasant to say the least. This is certainly true within one's own family,
but also at one's work at the office or in other workplaces.

Paul continues speaking to Timothy,

3 For the time will come when men will not put up with sound
doctrine. Instead, to suit their own desires, they will gather
around them a great number of teachers to say what their itching ears want to hear. 4 They will turn their ears away from the
truth and turn aside to myths. (2 Tim. 4:3-4).

Paul, among others, speaks here directly to all Christians, not only
to Timothy. At the same time, Paul speaks of situations we too are living
with. It occurs all around us, at work and likely in one's own family, or
local church. What is not receiving enough attention is about possible consequences for those involved in a sexual immoral lifestyle. Not
much, or not at all, attention is given to Bible verses such as: 1 Cor.
6:17-20; Gal. 5:19-21; James 1: 12-15; Jude 1:7; Rev. 21:8.

Holy Fear versus Human Feelings
The overall concern I wish to share at the end of our discussion on immorality is the spiritual decline in too many local church communities.
That personal concern has even deepened because in many discussions
about immorality, hardly any reference is made to God's Word with its

binding truth. This lack of acknowledgment concerning God's much-repeated view about immorality, raises serious concerns about the future of many denominations in North America.

Why is it that the numerous references to the Bible concerning issues of immoral behavior have been sorely omitted? How many Bible verses are not pointing out that Christians are wrong in their conclusion that personal *feelings* determine what choices to make in their lives, not realizing the grave consequences of their actions against the will of their Creator.

From the Bible we learn that it is not about one's feeling, but about one's obedience to Jesus, the living Word, to the One who gave His life on the cross, thereby giving true, un-swerving believers much desire and much needed spiritual power to live God-pleasing, God-obedient lives unto everlasting life on a renewed world.

The question we may raise at this point why and how it comes that so many Christians seem less concerned, or having less or no concern at all about the consequence of disobeying Jesus than about obeying their personal feelings and the right to do what they feel and want to do. Such a destructive mindset and behavior demonstrate no consideration, no willingness, to seek the help from the Holy Spirit in handling their feelings and thoughts how to live God-pleasing lives. The much-needed question that needs to be raised is why and precisely what drives one to circumvent Jesus' personally expressed will? (Rev. 2 and Rev. 22).

An answer to that hovering, unsettling question can be found in the fact that they live with fear, plain human fear. It is a fear that comes when one stands up for the truth that could have consequences. We are living within a world that is very tough on those who live by the truth found only in the Bible. We are living in a world that is growing steadily in opposing God, thereby seriously opposing those who live according to what the Bible tells us how to live Christ-pleasing lives. Many Christians are finding out that living world-pleasing, world-accommodating lives is far more convenient than Christ-pleasing lives. Such a truth is applied at work, among friends, within families, and even in churches.

These days, many Christians are afraid of and/or resist facing the consequences of standing up for Jesus by living a God-pleasing lifestyle.

It is up to church leadership to realize that some, or even many church members need helpful support in terms of prayer, understanding, and healing through the power of the Holy Spirit. That is being a living, obedient church within a world that has turned its back to God and thereby, unknowingly, will reap the consequences of that behavior, including lack of peace, turmoil and confusion in various ways.

Regarding '*lack of fear of the Lord*,' please read Genesis 6: 11-13; Numbers 14:9 (fill in 'people of the world we live in); Psalm 34:1-4; Proverbs 1:7; 8:13; 9:19; Ecclesiastes 8:11-13, Matthew 18:1-4, Romans 3:10-18.

Again, see APPENDIX A for personal reflection and small-group discussions on the subject concerned.

Small groups
It is recommended and encouraged to form small groups within local churches. It is within small groups of Christ-obedient, Christ-loving and trusting Christians that much needed spiritual power can be released to help those who may struggle due to sinful feelings or behavior. Small groups should be at the heart of any church community, now more than ever before, as we live in the so called 'End Times.' Don't forget, Satan is moving fast and furiously to undermine and dissolve church communities, and families as well. Those sad realities have already happened in Western Europe more than 30 years ago. My wife Louisa and I (Peter) have seen this fist hand in the Netherlands during the 1990s.[25]

What seems to be missing in discussions and conversations concerning immoral lifestyles is a serious, much needed reflection on what the Bible tells us, for example, about immorality. APPENDIX A could be used for reflection and discussions on the subject concerned.

Shortly after writing earlier on the words under the heading, "Holy Fear versus Human Feelings," I read the following words from Martin Luther written to a friend of the Reformation,

---

[25] Joep De Hart, "*ZWEVENDE GELOVIGEN: Oude Religie en Nieuwe Spiritualiteit*," (transl. "DRIFTING/WONDERING BELIEVERS: Old Religion and New Spirituality"), published by Bert Bakker, Amsterdam, 2011, ISBNN: 9789037706444.

We cannot attain to the understanding of Scripture either by study or by the intellect. Your first duty is to begin with prayer. Entreat the Lord to grant you, of His great mercy, the true understanding of His word. There is no other interpreter of the Word of God than the Author of this Word, as He Himself has said, 'They shall be all taught of God.' Hope for nothing from your own labors, from your own understanding: trust solely in God, and in the influence of His Spirit. Believe this on the word of a person who has had such an experience.

Then the same author who wrote the above words of Luther, also said,

Here is a lesson of vital importance to those who feel that God has called them to present to others the solemn truths for this time. These truths will stir the enmity of Satan and of men who love the fables that he has devised. In the conflict with the powers of evil there is need of something more than strength of intellect and human understanding. When enemies appealed to custom and tradition, or to the assertions and authority of the pope, Luther met them with the Bible and the Bible only.[26]

Proponents of immoral lifestyles need to be met with the Bible and the Bible only! Listen to what Jesus said,

My teaching is not my own. It comes from Him who sent Me. If anyone chooses to do God's will find out whether My teaching comes from God or whether I speak on My own. (John 7: 16-17).

In addition to the above words, we read in John 7 that we also may listen to what Psalm 119:5 says,

---

[26] E. G. White, *THE GREAT CONTROVERSY*, 2017 Remnant Publications, Inc., Project Restore, Inc. CELEBRATING THE 500 ANNIVERSARY of the Great Protestant Reformation.

"Oh, that my ways were steadfast in obeying your decrees!

Then we read in the same Psalm these words,

Teach me, O LORD, to follow Your decrees; then I will keep
them to the end. Give me understanding, and I will keep Your
law and obey it with all my heart. (Ps. 119:33-34).

Jesus sternly warns us in Revelation 2 and 22, that we should avoid
any expression of immorality, and that we need to listen and to obey
Him! If not, the same Psalm 119 reminds us that if we are not steadfast
in obeying Him, we will have to deal with the consequences. One of the
consequences is found in James 4:2, "*You want something but don't get it.*"
Think about what that 'something' could mean.

Once again, we hear God's word speaking to us about immorality and principles Christians should live by, as is underscored by Greg
Bahnsen in his book, HOMOSEXUALITY: A Biblical View.[27] In this
book Bahnsen reminds his readers that,

studies about homosexuality instruct the moralist to keep in
mind the distinction between homosexual activity and the homosexual condition...There is a difference between external
homosexual behavior and some inner factor, variously called a
"predisposition, orientation, psychic condition, constitution,
propensity," etc. (pp.63, 64).

Bahnsen responds to the outcome of such studies as follows:

The Bible does not say anything about sexual *orientation*, which
is the subject of modern discussions. Such a premise is faulty in
at least two ways.

First, it seems to suppress the relevant that the primary
Author of Scripture was God Himself, who is omniscient, and

---

[27] Greg L. Bahnsen, "*Homosexuality: a biblical view,*" Baker Book House Company,
1978. ISBN: 0-8010-0744-5.

therefore does not need to have His revealed will in Scripture replaced, or qualified by modern psychological guidance…the fact remains that He does not distinguish between acceptable and unacceptable aspects of homosexuality in Scripture, and in Scripture is to be found everything sufficient for "training in righteousness, that the man of God may be fully equipped for every good work."

Second, Scripture teaches that all men inherit a depraved, fleshly nature, as follows:

- A principle of sin operates in their members and captivates them (Rom. 7:23).
- The fleshly nature brings forth fruit unto death (Rom. 7:5),
- It lusts against the Spirit so that men cannot do the things they would. (Gal. 5:17).
- The flesh gives rise to certain forms of evil (Gal. 5:19).
- By nature, men fulfill the desires of the flesh and mind (Eph. 2:3).
- Out of the heart are the issues of life, (Prov. 4:23),
- The Bible portrays man's heart as stiff, crooked, uncircumcised, deceitful, divided, hard, blind, and darkened. (Deut. 10:16; Prov. 17:20; Jer. 9:26; 17:9; Hos. 10:2. Matt. 19:8; Eph. 4:18).
- A man's psychological predisposition is calloused (Eph. 4:19) and defiled (Titus 1:15) and in his mind against God and cannot be otherwise (Rom. 8:7; Col. 1:21).
- Men are drawn away by their own lusts, which conceived and bring forth sin (James 15:19).
- Out of the heart proceed evil thoughts, murders, adulteries, fornications, thefts, false witness, blasphemies" (Matt. 15:19)
- Inner traits or disposition such as: lack of self-control, soon angry, having feet swift to shed blood, being presumptuous and self-willed, having eyes full of adultery that cannot cease from sin, being stubborn and obstinate. (Rom. 8:7;

Col. 1:21; James 1:14, 15), 2 Tim. 3:3. Prov. 14:17; 16:32; Rom. 3:15; Isa. 59:7; 2 Pet. 2:10, 14; Ezek. 2:4).

I (Peter) wish to close this contribution to the discussion on immorality by repeating the final words of Jesus in Rev. 22,

4 Blessed are those who wash their robes, that they may have the right to the tree of life and may go through the gates into the city... 15 Outside are the dogs, those who practice magic arts, the sexually immoral, the murderers, the idolaters and everyone who loves and practices falsehood.

Following those final words of Jesus, we listen to the final words of serious warning spoken by the Spirit-inspired John at the closing of the Bible,

19 "And if anyone takes words away from this book of prophesy, God will take away from him his share in the tree of life and in the holy city, which are described in this book." (Rev. 22:19).

The above-mentioned warning from Jesus is captivated by the well-known story about the complete destruction of Sodom and Gomorrah, told in Genesis 19. In that story we hear of two angels urging Lot and his family to flee from the city of Sodom to escape the wrath of God on that city. In his comments on that story, Pastor Dan Jongsma exhorts his readers as follows,

God's exhortation still stands: flee from evil! Flee, before evil gets its claws so deeply embedded into you that you are unable to break free. Running from sin is not the mark of a coward, but yielding to sin is. It takes guts to admit our vulnerability and to flee from sin's overwhelming power. There is a high price in choosing to follow Jesus—but a higher price in not choosing to follow Him.[28]

---

[28] Dan Jongsma, Christian Reformed Church North America's 'TODAY,' July/August 2023 Issue.

The bottom line is that Christians need to remain true to the Lord in all circumstances, though having to face difficult situations. One example of facing a difficult situation came on July 24, 2023, illustrated in the following announcement below,

United Nations Threatens Canada's Christian Rights
July 24, 2023,

A storm is brewing at the United Nations… It's a challenge to our right to practice our Christian beliefs, and it's happening now. Recently, during the 53rd United Nations Human Rights Council (UNHRC), a report was released that claims religious freedom conflicts with LGBT rights. It suggests that governments should enforce acceptable LGBT standards within religious contexts and penalize non-compliant religious leaders and organizations. Make no mistake… This report isn't just a recommendation, it's a blueprint for governments to control religious practices and enforce LGBT ideologies within religious settings.

This means that Canada has become an unsafe place for Christians. The above-mentioned alarming effects of this notice could reach far and wide - from your local priest or pastor to your kids at university, and even you, as reader! Expressing your opinions based on your religious beliefs could potentially result in being reported.

Public Endorsement of Immoral Behavior
Two Examples

Example 1: Maine LGBT Group Defines Heterosexuals as 'Breeders' on School Poster Outside a Classroom, By Alice Giordano December 28, 2022, Updated: December 28, 2022

A publicly-funded poster of LGBT definitions hung in public schools across Maine defines heterosexuals as "breeders."

Example 2: General Motors Funds Transgenderism Efforts in Children's Classrooms By Bryan Jung January 1, 2023, Updated: January 1, 2023

General Motors (GM) provided a grant to a pro-transgender organization that supplies kindergarten and elementary classrooms with children's books that support its ideology.

The Detroit-based automaker made a donation last year to the Gay Lesbian and Straight Education Network's (GLSEN) "Rainbow Library" Program, according to its 2021 Social Impact Report (pdf).

The GM report admitted to funding the "Rainbow Library's" efforts to provide "supportive curriculum materials and book sets that are LGBTQ+ centered, racially diverse, and multicultural to K-12 schools."

"This innovative program also provides ongoing support and professional guidance for educators to create inclusive, supportive and identity-safe classrooms nationwide," it continued.   (next page)

GM did not mention how much money was awarded to the pro-transgender group, but did provide "$86.7 million in cash and in-kind donations to non-profits working to help create inclusive solutions to social issues around the world" in 2021, according to the report. In addition to children's books, the organization has been trying to influence school math departments with articles like "How Do We Make Math Class More Inclusive of Trans and Non-Binary Identities?"

"In recent years, GM and Chevrolet have provided grants to GLSEN to support their work to create safe, supportive and LGBTQ-inclusive learning environments for students. This is just one of the many initiatives and causes that GM has supported, as the company provides philanthropic grants to hundreds of non-profits each year," wrote a spokeswoman for GM and Chevrolet to The Epoch Times.

Public Announcements on Changing
Social Matters
   Examples taken from News Outlets
   Elizabeth Johnston from Faith, Family, Freedom, February 7, 2023
3.1.1.2. Singers Sam Smith and Kim Petras caused a stir during Sunday night's performance of the song "Unholy" at the Grammy's that was rife with overt Satanic imagery and raunchy sexual suggestiveness. The two would go on to make history as the first "non-binary" and transgender person, respectively, to win the award for best pop duo.

Gregory Metz, CitizenGO, February 7, 2023 Drag Queen Story Time in schools and libraries across Canada as normal education content

The Epoch Times, February 7, 2023
Topic: 'What the Chinese regime is Hiding from the World?'
"The Final War" is a must-see documentary exposing China's deadly plan for the free world. It offers the American public profound wisdom about the future of our nation's families, children, and individuals by presenting the best understanding of the CCP's severe penetration of the United States and the Western World.

The Epoch Times, February 8, 2023
Topic: 'Ontario Catholic Student Arrested as Gender Belief Controversy Escalates.'
Josh Alexander, 16, was arrested for attending St. Joseph's High School in Renfrew, Ont., on Monday. The principal had recently banned him from school grounds because he said he would continue to express his belief that God created only two genders.
The notice lists things Alexander has refused to do that have led to his exclusion. He has refused to use pronouns or names that are inconsistent with students' biological sex. He has refused to refrain from freely professing that people cannot change gender and that "boys must not be permitted to enter girls' private spaces as a matter of morality, modesty, and safety."
His lawyer, James Kitchen, told The Epoch Times, "He's not a belligerent kid and this isn't about him getting his 15 minutes of fame. This is about principle. It's about beliefs. Josh was not going to tacitly condone the religious segregation."

The Epoch Times, February 8, 2023
Topic: 'Look at the Devil behind the Grammys Curtain'
Commentary
Satanism suddenly seems to be everywhere. But don't worry, the real problem, we're told, is noticing it.

In the wake of the revolting Grammy Awards performance of the song "Unholy" from singers Sam Smith and Kim Petras on Feb. 5, Page Six had this to say: "Conservative commentators took issue with Sam Smith's hell-themed performance at the 2023 Grammys, with some going so far as to describe it as 'satanic.'"

Who could possibly think that a quasi-pornographic, hell-themed performance portraying devil worship and sexual sadism could possibly be satanic? Well, anyone frankly. And the Grammys performance was but one more log on the hellfire.

Examples of overtly satanic imagery lately are legion. Who can forget Satan-themed sneakers marketed to teens with satanic symbols and human blood? More recently, Vanity Fair collaborated with Madonna on a blasphemous photoshoot making a mockery of the Last Supper.

In a very on-brand move, The Satanic Temple is set to open a free abortion clinic where they can perform in droves what they claim to be their religious abortion ritual. This ritual includes reciting their sacred tenets, such as "One's body is inviolable, subject to one's own will alone."

Such tenets echo Aleister Crowley, the father of modern satanism, who famously announced,

"Do what thou wilt shall be the whole of the law." In the world of the occult, Lucifer is considered the perennial light-bearer, and God the ultimate oppressor. Freedom from oppression in this construct requires never subordinating one's will to the will of God. The Devil doesn't ask upfront for fidelity to him, but rather simply for fidelity to self. "Thy will be done" becomes "My will be done."

Sheila Gunn Reid, February 8, 2023
Grade 11 student banned from school for the year for 'bullying' trans peers by being Catholic,

Josh Alexander, a Renfrew Ontario St Joseph's Catholic High School student, was suspended for 20 days in late 2022 for expressing the accepted Catholic view in class and on social media that there are only two genders. On the 25th of November, students at St. Joseph's Catholic High School in Renfrew will be walking out. Join us at the intersection of Barnet Blvd and 1st St. All are welcome. Please keep traffic moving. This walkout may be postponed if the CUPE strike interferes.

Sheila Gunn Reid, February 13, 2023, Topic: Mental Health and MAID: Canadians question looming changes to Canada's assisted-death law Just three-in-ten (31%) say they support the concept of offering MAID for irremediable mental illness. Half (51%) oppose this idea. Justice Minister David Lametti said in early February that the additional one-year delay (the government previously requested a two-year pause on expansion) will "provide time to help provincial and territorial partners and the medical and nursing communities to prepare to deliver MAID in these circumstances."

The Banner, March 3, 2023.
Topic: Christian Reformed Church Among Those Lamenting 'Hastened Death' in Canada,

Al Postma, transitional executive director-Canada for the Christian Reformed Church in North America, was one of 51 Christian ministry leaders to sign a "Christian Leaders Statement" organized by the Evangelical Fellowship of Canada against hastened death by medical means. The Canadian government refers to this as "medical assistance in dying."

> "As followers of Jesus, we share a deep and profound commitment to the sanctity of all human life," the statement says. "Human life is being devalued and discarded when people in vulnerable situations among us are not being supported to live but facilitated to die."

Since 2016, Canada has had legislation granting access to medical assistance to end one's life for individuals experiencing "intolerable suffering" and for whom there was a "reasonable foreseeability of natural death." After constitutional challenges, that stipulation is no longer required and the choice of MAID is available "to relieve intolerable suffering, regardless of proximity to natural death."

The law is set to expand again to make the program available to those for whom the suffering is not physical but mental illness, but that legislation has been delayed.

In October the Evangelical Fellowship of Canada presented the following statement to its members and partners released on Feb. 21,

We lament hastened death in Canada. We grieve the expansion in law that has made those whose death is not reasonably foreseeable eligible for hastened death, and that soon will include people with mental illness as their only underlying medical condition," the letter says.

The above statement affirms several things that include the love of God for all persons; the duty of care we owe to one another; the importance of holistic care; and that love, care, and comfort are the appropriate responses to suffering. "We advocate," the signers say, "for universally accessible, high-quality palliative care for those facing life-limiting diagnosis or nearing death; for accessible and adequate services and support for Canadians living with disability, chronic illness or mental illness, including safe, secure and affordable housing; for better home care and extended care; and for the protection of conscience for those who cannot accept hastened.

Euthanasie Prevention Coalition.
James Schadenberg,

Topic: Government report recommends euthanasia for children and euthanasia by advanced directive. February 16, 2023.

A report by the Special Joint Committee on Medical Assistance in Dying (AMAD) was tabled in the House of Commons on February 15 calling for a drastic expansion of euthanasia (MAID) in Canada. The report recommends that children "mature minors" and patients with mental illnesses should be eligible for euthanasia and that patients with illnesses such as dementia should be permitted to make advanced requests by advanced directives for euthanasia.

The Epoch Times July 10, 2023
When They Say, 'We're Coming for Your Children,' Believe Them. Barbara Kay,

For years, Canadians have proved amenable to demands for basic rights, but also to entitlements, for those who identify, variously, as "trans," "non-binary" or "queer." These entitlements, even those encroaching on women's rights, are supported by government and most media. They extend into all our cultural, therapeutic, and social institutions.

The only domain in which we are witnessing a groundswell of citizen resistance is K–12 pedagogy, where Queer Theory—a gendered form of Marxism that rejects the "normal" in sexuality, including the notion of childhood "innocence"—is systematically imposed on vulnerable minds, with or without parental consent. Drag Queen Story Hour (DQSH) has become the cynosure of parental disquiet.

A recent video clip of naked Pride marchers chanting "We're here, we're queer, we're coming for your children" went viral. LGBTQ spin doctors claimed the words were "taken out of context." Which begs the question of why male drag queens no longer stay in their lane of adult entertainment. What acceptable "context" encourages teaching children to "twerk" ("you just move your bum up and down like that")—an action simulating sexual intercourse?

Left-wing Abortion Program

Canadian Liberal leader Susan Holt has been promoting her LGBT ideology in the provincial election in New Brunswick, October 2024. As part of her plans to create more access to abortion centres she tried to lift restrictions on funding private, for-profit abortion centres. However, due to the prayers and activism of Campaign Life Coalition (CLC) supporters other NB pro-lifers, and a pivotal 40 Days of Life campaign outside the facility organized by a former CLC intern, Clinic 554 had shut its doors for good earlier last years. (CLC NATIONAL NEWS: Campaign Life Coalition Canada, May 2025).

Spiritual Warfare

In a final word on this very serious and confrontational subject of immorality, I (Peter) wish to share some final thoughts about the tragedy enfolding before our eyes on this subject. This very subject is causing a serious division in many local churches that may lead, and has already led, to splits in local churches. Many members have already left their local church altogether, which happened in our local church earlier this year (2025).

Well, be aware! As already mentioned earlier, Satan is very experienced in how and by what means he will be successful in creating an atmosphere within families and churches, thereby cleverly uses what we may call conditioning, i.e. learning to live with one another despite serious disagreements. Many will gravitate to that idea of living together, while disagreeing with each other. Keeping peace is all that counts, as it sounds quite Christian, isn't it? However, what is suffering in such a scenario is the truth, as it also means throwing Jesus serious warning in the wind.

Speaking of suffering, we may pay close attention to what Paul writes regarding Living Sacrifices in Romans 12,

> 1 Therefore, I urge you, brothers, in view of God's mercy, to offer your bodies as living sacrifices, holy and pleasing to God—this is your spiritual act of worship. 2 Do not conform any longer to the pattern of this world but be transformed by the renewing of your mind. Then you will be able to test and approve what God's will is—His good, pleasing and perfect will. (Rom. 12:1, 2).

When the Rubber Hits the Road

Considering well-meant efforts to keep the peace in families and within the local church, we may listen to what Jesus has to say on the matter of keeping peace among each other despite serious disagreements concerning the truth mentioned in Matt. 10,

> Do not suppose that I have come to bring peace to the earth. I did not come to bring peace, but a sword. For I have come to turn a man against his father, a daughter against her mother, a

daughter-in-law against her mother-in-law — a man's enemies will be the members of his own household.(Matt. 10:34)

Jesus words above weren't spoken specifically about immoral behaviour, but they can still be applied to our discussion. We shouldn't dismiss them offhand, as immorality within the context of a family or a local church is a serious matter – and was most certainly in Jesus' mind. He addresses this issue more directly in Revelation 2:14, 20, and Revelation 22:15. Let us hold on to the truth spoken by the Living Truth, Jesus Christ, at the very end of the Bible! This is a most-important fact never to be ignored or dismissed.

From the book, *The Great Controversy*, we read the following lines about truth,

Truth is no more desired by the majority today than it was by the papist who opposed Luther. There is the same disposition to accept the theories and traditions of men instead of the word of God as in former ages. Those who present the truth for this time should not expect to be received with greater favor than were earlier reformers. The great controversy between truth and error, between Christ and Satan, is to increase in intensity to the close of this world's history.[29]

Walking in Lockstep with Jesus

In today's Western societies we, Christians, are more than ever before challenged to walk in lockstep with Jesus. That means we are following the guidelines the Bible gives us. Especially when the Western world seems to follow the rules set by those who, at best, ignore the standards of living clearly explained in the Bible. That includes standards concerning moral behavior Jesus Himself and all Spirit-inspired contributors to God's word, the Bible, have addressed this subject of sexual immorality!

Those who want to walk in lockstep with Jesus may take note of the short Bible passage taken from 1 Corinthians 5, 11,

---

[29] E.G White, *The Great Controversy*, Celebrating The 500th Anniversary of the Great Protestant Reformation, 7 Remnant Publications, Inc., 2017.

"I (Paul) writing you that you must not associate with anyone who calls himself a brother but is sexual immoral or greedy, an idolater or a slanderer, a drunkard or a swindler. With such a man do not even eat. (1 Cor. 5:11).

This one Bible verse expresses the meaning of 'walking in lockstep with Jesus' considering living and applying a moral standard. Such a standard is expected in the life of any church community. As an example, such a biblical rule needs to be applied in church worship during the time of the Lord Supper celebration. Churches that are open to those living in a homosexual relationship need to be aware that some of them could take the chance to take part in the Lord Supper celebration. By God's standards, that should not happen.

Walking in lockstep with Jesus is about living a Christian rhythm that expresses faith in Jesus no matter what difficult situation you must deal with. In the Bible book Hebrews, we find the following encouraging words in Chapter 12,

2 "Let us fix our eyes on Jesus, the author and perfecter of our faith, who for the joy set before Him endured the cross, scorning its shame, and sat down at the right hand of the throne of God. 3 Consider Him who endured such opposition from sinful men, so that you will not grow weary and lose heart." (Hebr.12:2, 3).

The reality of Satan's influence

We all need to realize the position of Satan. First, Satan had been created as one of many angels. He became one of the strongest if not the strongest angel, and as such got it in his mind to oppose God, his Creator, to the point of trying to overthrow and to replace God. At that point, God threw him out of the heavenly sphere towards the earth.

Jesus recalled that event as we can read in the Gospel of Luke, Chapter 10. We read in this chapter,

1 "The Lord appointed seventy-two and sent them two-by-two ahead of Him to every town and place where He was about to go…17 The seventy-two returned with joy and said, "Lord, even the demons submit to us in Your name." 18 He (Jesus) replied, "I saw Satan fall like lightning from heaven." (Lk. 10:1, 17-18a).

At the time Satan, then a fallen angel, or demon, was thrown out of heaven onto the earth inhabited by Adam and Eve. Read Genesis 1:26-27, Genesis 2:4-25. In Genesis 3 we hear about Satan, then characterized as a serpent, who succeeded in convincing Eve and then Adam to eat from the tree in the middle of the garden they were warned by God not to eat from. As a result of listening to Satan and not to God they were to die. Death became part of us, human beings.

Thus, we hear that 'There is a malevolent entity in the world, whose influence is felt at virtually every level of society. That entity is Satan, the devil.' This truth concerning Satan is overwhelmingly present in today's world, as it is a hugely destructive force at work in the many disciplines and sectors in our Western societies. We see and hear about the results of Satan's ongoing and growing influence, not the least concerning growing sexual immorality.

This issue of sexual immorality is plaguing Christian families and relationships. I know of a denomination that has 30% of her membership accepting this immoral behavior. It could well be that such high percentage is true within many denominations. Such a fact demonstrates the growing influence within Christianity, which is deeply concerning, as we realize that Satan is not backing off. Such a reality brings us back to what Jesus has said in Revelation 22, where we read,

12 "Behold, I am coming soon! My reward is with me, and I will give to everyone according to what he has done. 13 I am the Alpha and the Omega, the First and the Last, the Beginning and the End. 14 Blessed are those who wash their robes, that they may have the right to the tree of life and may go through the gates into the city. 15 Outside are the dogs, those

who practice magic arts, the **sexually immoral**, the murderers, the idolaters, and everyone who loves and practices falsehood. (Rev. 22:14-15).

Then, following the above-written words of Jesus, we hear the Spirit-inspired John saying as a warning for all Christians,

19 And if anyone takes words away from this book of prophecy, God will take away from him his share in the tree of life and in the holy city, which are described in this book. (Rev. 22:19).

What has been said above by Jesus Himself and Spirit-inspired words spoken by John, as well as other contributors to the Bible concerning sexual immoral behavior, should take those words of a serious warning far above the words that elevates one's personal feelings above the Word of God! Please do not throw Jesus' serious warning in the wind, as that will lead to serious consequences concerning well or not living eternal life with Jesus Christ.

Note: Read also verses such as Genesis 2:4—3:20.

Significance of the Redefinition of Marriage

Finally, the subject of marriage is important to look at in our discussion on immoral behavior. In today's world, marriage has become a contentious issue and therefore it is helpful to hear what Hank Hanegraaff (CRI- Bible Answer Man - Hank Unplugged Short) has to say about the meaning and value of marriage. Marriage, Hanegraaff says, is certainly not a 'figment of imagination,' but a precious God-given creational gift to mankind to grow, expand and to be a blessing.

Jan 9, 2023, Hank Hanegraaff, president of the Christian Research Institute and host of the Bible Answer Man broadcast, explains why the redefinition of marriage is such a serious matter. In the considered opinions of such great western philosophers as Socrates, Plato, and Aristotle, marriage was seen as a relationship between men and women. Indeed, in the Judeo-Christian tradition marriage has always been rooted in the dual, gender-distinct nature of humanity. As such, intercourse consummates marriage as a multifaceted mystery in which two people are forged together as one flesh. In mysterious union, a man and a woman procreate children fashioned in the image and likeness of their Creator.

Marriage, however, is even more profound than procreation and paradisiacal pleasure—it is a mysterious parable of Christ and His Church. The union of two people poignantly portrays the unity of Christ and His bride. The parable has its roots in Genesis and bears ultimate fruit in Revelation. There are essentially three building blocks of civil society—marriage, church, government—resting atop the foundation of human life. Of the three none is more significant than marriage.

The ABC'S—Anthropology: women and men enjoy strategic complementarity; as such, both are essential in the rearing of children. Biology: sexual reproduction requires male and female. Civics: Redefining marriage opens Pandora's Box and spells the death knell to civil society.

The following two examples reminds us of the possibility that someone involved in sexual immoral behavior can get out of that God-opposing and denying reality and to live a God-pleasing life.

The theme of this book: 'HOPE amidst Hopelessness' is well expressed in the following two examples:

Two Abbreviated Stories.

First example
Why I'm Not Pursuing Gay Relationships Anymore
Mar 14, 2017
In the thick of our disagreement that night, God planted this thought in my head: "Why don't you investigate this matter for yourself and come to your own conclusions?"......

As I re-examined the arguments that said Scripture permits loving gay relationships, I found that they weren't as convincing as I had initially thought when I first came across them. I discovered many loopholes in those claims. I began to move away from gay-affirming theology, as God used numerous occasions to solidify the conviction in my heart that homosexuality was not aligned to His will. ......

I saw that the Word of God consistently referred to Jesus as *the Bridegroom* (male) (Mark 2:19-20, John 3:29) and the Church as *His Bride* (female) (Matthew 25:1-13, Revelation 21:2; 9-10), and that the consummation of history was described as the Wedding Feast of the Lamb of God (Revelation 19:9). This sealed the conviction in my heart that God has created us *male* and *female* for very good reasons (Genesis 5:2)…...

Those seven years of searching and researching were life changing…. Although I started out being gay-affirming and had no interest whatsoever in changing my stand on homosexuality, the Hol y Spirit planted and deepened the conviction in my heart over the years about God's wonderful design for my sexuality.

Comments/in Everyday Living, Identity, TOPICS/by Raphael Zhang

Second Example

My So-Called Ex-Gay Life By Gabriel Arana

April 11, 2012

Instead of fire-and-brimstone denunciations from the pulpit, the ex-gay movement allowed the Christian right to couch its condemnation of homosexuality in a way that seemed compassionate. Focus on the Family called its new ex-gay ministry "Love Won Out" and talked about healing and caring for homosexuals.…...

Two largest groups that provide ex-gay counseling are Exodus International, a nondenominational Christian organization, and NARTH, its secular counterpart. If Exodus is the spirit of the ex-gay movement, NARTH is the brain.…...

Nicolosi remains NARTH's most visible advocate. Exodus had 83 chapters in 34 states. Its president, Alan Chambers, claimed in 2004 that he knew "tens of thousands of people who have successfully changed their sexual orientation".…...

Nicolosi encouraged me to interpret my daily life through the lens of his theories. I read in one of Nicolosi's books, *Reparative*

Therapy of Male Homosexuality, that he tries to position himself as a supportive father figure, typifying the sort of relationship that he believes his patients never had with their own father. I indeed came to see him this way.

As I progressed in therapy, I felt that I was gaining insight into the source and causes of my sexual attractions.

ANTICIPATED
END-TIME DEVELOPMENTS

CHAPTER FOUR
TIME-RESTRICTED PLANET EARTH

Genesis

In Genesis, Chapter One, we learn about the creation of the heavens and the earth, and at the end of God's creation story we read about the creation of the first two human beings, Adam and Eve, as follows,

> 26 Then God said, "Let us make man in our image, in our likeness. So, God created man in His own image, in the image of God He created him; male and female He created them. (Gen. 1:26).

Then in verse 31 we read,

> God saw all that He had made, and it was very good. (Gen. 1:31).

The two above quoted Bible verses help us understand that the first human beings were created without a sinful nature. Then, in Chapter Three, we read how these first two same people became sinful persons as they disobeyed god's warning, as we read in the following passage.

In Genesis, Chapter Three, we learn about the Fall of Adam and Eve, as they threw God's warning in the wind *not to eat the fruit from the tree in the middle of the garden* (vs. 3). In the following verses we read how the serpent (Gen. 3:1), also referred to as the devil or Satan, succeeded in convincing both human beings to eat from the one tree standing in the middle of the Garden of Eden, though God had warned them not to eat from that one particular 'tree of life.' As a result, both Adam and Eve, became sinners and lost their chance to live forever. That historic fact led to the sinful nature of all following generations.

From God's Word we understand that at one time Satan, in his position of archangel, desired all power for himself and dared to challenge God to take the overall control over creation, including Planet Earth. God then simply threw Satan out of heaven unto Planet Earth. In Luke 10:18, Jesus said to the seventy-two, who had returned to Jesus overjoyed that they had experienced, how even the demons had submitted to them, saying,

I saw Satan fall like lightning from heaven. (Lk. 10:18).

Planet Earth **is unique, as scientists have found this planet to be the only planet to have liquid water on its surface, intelligent life-forms living on it, a sun and a moon that helps regulate surface temperatures, an atmosphere with 21 percent oxygen and plate tectonics, according to Space.com.** Scientists believe that the Earth exists in a "Goldilocks zone" where conditions are just right to support life. In addition, the sun radiates <u>energy</u> mainly as <u>light</u>, <u>ultraviolet</u> and <u>infrared</u> radiation, and is the most important source of energy for <u>life</u> on <u>Earth</u>. (Information taken from the internet).

At that moment in time, the earth was in a state as described in Genesis 1, that Satan, after his fall unto earth, was bound to stay on earth. He was on earth before Adam and Eve were created. As a supreme deceiver, serpent Satan succeeded in deceiving Eve and Adam to eat from the tree they were not supposed to eat from, as we read earlier. From that time on, we may speak of a fallen Planet Earth, i.e. a fallen, sinful world facing a future destruction.

As we are living in a time-restricted world/earth we learn from the Bible that at a certain time in the future this fallen world/earth, together with all of creation, will not only be destroyed, but then also completely renewed. At that time, present heavens will be renewed as well. After the complete renewal of heavens and earth, Jesus will return to the renewed planet earth together with His Church. More on this subject in Chapter Eight.

Jesus about the End of the Age

It seems appropriate to start this last book of the trilogy, *THE ROYAL DEAL*, with words Jesus Christ used in the Gospels to describe the End Times. Then we will also pay attention to a number of actual occurrences we experience in today's world as part of the End Times. Notice hereby that Jesus is speaking to a predominant Jewish audience.

Before turning to several Bible passages, it is helpful to realize that,

   a. The Bible passage of Luke 21 is quite like Matthew 24:1-35 and Mark 13:1-30. Then there are also similar Bible passages between Matthew 24:36-44 and Mark 13:32-37.

   b. From Robert H. Gundry's commentary on MATTHEW (1982) we learn that Matthew had taken over Marcan material concerning international upheaval and natural disasters with his main interest in the persecution of disciples and the rise of antinomianism in the church.

   c. The Bible passage Mark 13 entitled 'The Olivet Discourse," is part of the so called Marcan outline including Jesus' Ministry, culminating in the conflict with the Temple authorities.[30]

Howard Marshall's 'COMMENTARY on LUKE informs us that Luke's narrative 'Signs of the End of the Age' (Luke 21:5-28) is similar in form to that in Mark, though the wording differs, and the scene is different. He assumes that Luke is using Mark's narrative as Gundry does. Thus, we will concentrate on Mark's report on wat Jesus has said about 'The End of the Age.'

Marriage at the Resurrection, Mark 12,

18 Then the Sadducees, who say there is no resurrection, came to Him with a question, 19 techerher, they said, "Moses wrote

---

[30] Instead of fire-and-brimstone denunciations from the pulpit, the ex-gay movement allowed the Christian right to couch its condemnation of homosexuality in a way that seemed compassionate. William L. Lane, *The Gospel of MARK*, William B. Eerdmans Publishing Company, 1974.

for us that if a man's brother dies and leaves his wife but no children, the man must marry the widow and have children for his brother. 20 Now there were seven brothers. The first one married and died without leaving any children. 21 The second one married the widow, but he also died, leaving no child. It was the same with the third.

22 In fact, none of the seven left any children. Last of all, the woman died too. 23 At the resurrection whose wife will she be, since the seven were married to her?" 24 Jesus replied, "Are you not in error because you do not know the Scriptures or the power of God? 25 When the dead rise, they will neither marry nor be *given* in marriage; they will be like the angels in heaven." (Mark 12:18-25).

Signs of the End of the Age (Mark 13)

1 As He was leaving the temple, one of His disciples said to Him, "Look, Teacher! What massive stones! What magnificent buildings!" 2 Do you see all these great buildings?" replied Jesus. "Not one stone here will be left on another; each one will be thrown down." As Jesus was sitting on the Mount of Olives opposite the temple, Peter, James, John and Andrew asked Him privately, 4 "Tell us, when will these things happen? And what will be the sign that they are all about to be fulfilled?"

5 Jesus said to them: "Watch out that no one deceives you. 6 Many will come in my name, claiming, 'I am He, and will deceive many. 7 When you hear of wars and rumors of wars, do not be alarmed. Such things must happen, but the end is still to come. 8 Nation will rise against nation, and kingdom against kingdom. There will be earthquakes in various places, and famines. These are the beginning of birth pains. 9 You must be on your guard. You will be handed over to the stand before governors and kings as witnesses to them.

10 And the gospel must first be preached to all nations. 11 Whenever you are arrested and brought to trial, do not worry

beforehand about what to say. Just say whatever is given you at the time, for it is not you speaking, but the Holy Spirit.

12 Brother will betray brother to death, and the father his child. Children will rebel against their parents and have them put to death. 13 All men will hate you because of me, but he who stands firm to the end will be saved.

14 When you see 'the abomination that causes desolation' standing where it does not belong—let the reader understand—then let those who are in Judea flee to the mountains. 15 Let no one on the roof of his house go down or enter the house to take anything out. 16 Let no one in the field go back to get his cloak.

17 How dreadful it will be in those days for pregnant women and nursing mothers! 18. Pray that this will not take place in winter, 19 because those will be days of distress un equaled from the beginning, when God created the world, until now—and never to be equaled again.

20. If the Lord had not cut short those days, no one would survive. But for the sake of the elect, whom He has chosen, He has shortened them.

21 At that time if anyone says to you, 'Look, here is the Christ!' or, 'Look, there He is!' do not believe it. 22 For false Christs and false prophets will appear and perform signs and miracles to deceive the elect—if that were possible. 23 So be on your guard; I have told you everything ahead of time.

24 "But in those days' following that distress "'the sun will be darkened, and the moon will not give its light, 25 the stars will fall from the sky, and the heavenly bodies will be shaken.'

26 "At that time men will see the Son of Man coming in the clouds with great power and glory. 27 And He will send His angels and gather His elect from the four winds, from the ends of the earth to the ends of the heavens.

28 "Now learn this lesson from the fig tree. As soon as its twigs get tender and its leaves come out, you know that summer is near. 29 "Even so, when you see these things happening, you

know that it is near, right at the door. 30 "I tell you the truth, this generation will certainly not pass away until all these things have happened. 31 Heaven and earth will pass away, but my words will never pass away." (Mark 13:1-31).

The Day and Hour Unknown (Mark 13)

32 "No one knows about that day or hour, not even the angels in heaven, nor the Son, but only the Father. 33 Be on guard! Be alert! You do not know when that time come. 34 It's like a man going away. He leaves his house and puts his servants in charge, each with his assigned task, and tells the one at the door to keep watch, each with his assigned task, and tells the one at the door to keep watch.

35 "Therefore, keep watch because you do not know when the owner of the house will come back—whether in the evening, or at midnight, or when the rooster crows, or at dawn. 36 If he comes suddenly, do not let him find you sleeping. 37 What I say to you, I say to everyone: 'Watch!'" (Mk 13: 32-37).

Reflection

As indicated earlier, both Matthew and Luke used Mark's composition about the end times in their Gospels to describe the period of the end times. It seems that Jesus was explaining what the end times will look like, in both general and particular terms, though within the context of the nation Israel, as indicated by His reference to Judea, vs 14.

However, we must assume that He included the entire universe when He described the natural spectacles concerning the sun, moon and stars in verses 24-25.

Then also notice that Jesus spoke in verses 26 and 27 of the fact that at that time (all) men (people), including His elect from the four winds, from the ends of the earth to the ends of the heavens, will all see the Son of Man coming in the clouds with great power and glory.

Christians all over the world need to take note of the serious circumstances Jesus describes here in Mark's epistle. They all need to heed expressions such as: *Watch out that no one deceive you; do not be alarmed. Such things must happen; earthquakes in various places, and famines* (Mk. 13:5-8). Notice in the previous paragraph, vss. 26-27, that Jesus says that not only Christians, but the entire world (*all* men) will see Him descending with great power and glory. In our days we can imagine that such a momentous and world-significant event could most likely heard and watched through world-wide TV reporting, and even more so through smart phones almost everybody seems to have, and numerous times look at. Smart phones seem to be an essential part of life these days.

In Mark's 'Olivet Discourse' we read that there have been messianic pretenders during the first century who won momentary support, but those false messiahs were captured and killed. In verses 9-11 we hear about serious opposition from community leaders against those who dared to speak up for Jesus and would be killed if they did. In our present North American societies, we begin to sense that there is serious opposition to Christians who, for example, dare to say that forms of immoral lifestyles, such as sexual immorality and perversion, are wrong.

Paul, in his second letter to Timothy, warns Christians that,

12 "…everyone who wants to live a godly life in Christ Jesus will be persecuted, 13 while evil men and impostors will go from bad to worse, deceiving and being deceived. 14 But as for you, continue in what you have learned and have become convinced of…" (2 Tim. 3:12-14).

Timothy received this instruction at a time that the world, already then, was unraveling, apostasy was growing, and false teachers within the church were multiplying. In our present days, we need to take note of Paul's instructions to Timothy, so two thousand years later, in a world in which those, who dare to oppose immoral lifestyles, can expect some form of opposition and repercussion at work, within local churches and even within families. Such realities may well point out the growing influence of Satan in today's societies.

Satan's significant influence on the North American continent is following the same trend much earlier shown in Western Europe during the late-1970s to mid-1990s, when hundreds of churches per month were closed. We certainly can expect a similar trend in North America for quite some time to come. It is this trend that has been foreseen, as He had also foretold serious difficulties for His sincere followers, when we read Mark 13.

Commenting on Chapter 14, Professor Lane said that "The entire section, including verses 14-23, is to be interpreted in light of the events which occurred in the turbulent and chaotic period of AD 66-70." This period led eventually to Titus leading the Roman army,

> In surrounding the city of Jerusalem and began too slowly squeeze the life out of Jewish stronghold. By the year AD 70, the attackers had breached Jerusalem's outer walls and began a systematic ransacking of the city. The assault culminated in the burning and destruction of the Second Temple that served as the center of Judaism. In victory, the Romans slaughtered thousands. Of those sparred from death: thousands more were enslaved and sent to toil in the mines of Egypt, others were dispersed to arenas throughout the Empire to be butchered for the amusement of the public. The Temple's sacred relics were taken to Rome where they were displayed in celebration of the victory.[31]

Based on Mark 13:15-18, reference is made to Ezekiel 7:14-23.

The period of AD 66-70 led to the Second and final captivity/exile of the Jews from their homeland. That world-wide captivity/exile: AD 70 – AD 1948, led to the return of millions of Jews back to their home country after Israel was officially acknowledged and restored. That return continues even today.

Jesus is Ruling the Still Fallen World

---

[31] William L. Lane, *"The Gospel of MARK"* part of the series The New International Commentary on the New Testament, William B. Eerdmans Publishing Company, Grand Rapids, Michigan, p. 466. Reference: "The Romans Destroy the Temple of Jerusalem 70 AD," Eye Witness to History, www.eyewitnesstohistory.com (2005).

Different Views on Millennialism

Following is a discussion on three different opinions on a period of thousand years of prosperity during which Jesus Christ is expected to live and rule the world. These different opinions are described as Pre-millennialism, Post-millennialism and A-millennialism. These three different opinions are derived from Revelation 20:1-6. This discussion is primarily based on an in-depth study about thousand years by Dr. Christopher R. Smith.

Of these three different opinions Pre-millennialism seems to pay special attention to the existence of Israel as a separate state. As we think of Israel today as a separate state in the Middle East since 1948, we need to keep in mind that present-day Israelites are for the most part non-Christian people. Then you have the so-called Messianic Jews, living in many different countries, who believe in Jesus as their Lord and Savior based on the Bible.

In terms of their derivation, the three above-mentioned periods of millennialism refer to varying beliefs about the timing of Christ's Second Coming. They are supposed to answer the question when this event will take place relative to the millennium, i.e. a thousand-year era of worldwide peace, prosperity and justice described at the end of the book of Revelation.

Smith reminds us that from the 1600s to the early 1900s, the prevailing view among Protestants in Britain and America was that the Bible, being the inspired word of God, speaks of Christ as returning as King *after* the millennium. However, the world had not yet been transformed, as Christ would not have a kingdom to rule over. That meant that the millennium had to come first.

However, by the middle of the 1800s another view had developed in David Brown's 1858 book, entitled: *Christ's Second Coming: Will It Be Premillennial? That view explained that* Christ's return would be required to bring about the millennium, thus the term "premillennial." As *pre*-millennialism speaks of the belief that Christ's coming will be *pre*-millennial, *post*-millennialism is the belief that Christ's coming will *follow* the millennium. Then we also have the position that says that

Christ's coming will be *without* a millennium, which means that there will be no world-wide era of peace and justice at the end of history.

Besides the arguments about the period of the millennium, Smith argues that far more important are the beliefs about *how* the millennium will occur. That leads to the question what the millennium will be, given the fact that there will be no world-wide era of peace and justice at the end of history. While *pre*-millennialism is the belief that Christ's return will be required to bring about the millennium, *post*-millennialism is the belief that Christ's return will come as the culmination of the millennium, i.e. following the millennium.

Smith also explains that in this view, the kingdom of God is a *historical* reality as it comes *within* history. A-millennialism is the belief that Christ's return will take place without a millennium, since God does not intend to bring about a worldwide era of peace and justice on present earth (this is my (Peter's) view as well). However, Smith concludes that in this view the kingdom of God is a *spiritual* reality that stands *apart from* history. His conclusion is that all three possibilities are right, as the kingdom of God is a complex entity that has historical, eschatological, and spiritual aspects.

Smith further explains these different aspects by saying that the eschatological view dominated during the Roman persecutions, but the historical view largely displaced it when Constantine proclaimed himself to be a Christian emperor. Then, when Rome fell to barbarian invasions, the spiritual view came to the fore, exemplified by Augustine's great work *The City of God*. Smith explains the various millennial beliefs have practical applications as follows.

Premillennialism provides an eschatological understanding of the kingdom, thereby emphasizing *witness*. Postmillennialism, providing a historical understanding of the kingdom, tends to emphasize *service*, whereas a-millennialism, providing a more spiritual understanding of the kingdom, tends to emphasize *worship*. All three different understandings of millennialism are vital to the church's health and influence, as each of them provide valid insight into one aspect of the kingdom of God that underlies each one.

Smith is of the opinion that the historical expression of the kingdom of God (*post*-millennialism) is the one we need to pay most attention to, though he treasures the worship life of the church, and its ministry of word and sacrament as a mark of *a*-millennialism. However, the historical side of things requires intentionality, as it requires to get out of ourselves and into the world to see where we can make a difference by expressing our faith in what we believe Jesus wants us to do. Smith calls this "vocational postmillennialism."

Then, Smith further explains this kind of postmillennialism by saying that it entails the belief that as godly and sincere followers of Christ we need to pursue our divine calling with integrity into a variety of fields of human endeavor. With God's help we will rise to positions of influence that will allow us to shape the society and culture around them.

Having followed Smith's reflection on the three different positions on millennialism, I personally prefer the position of a-millennialism. A-millennialism, next to the importance of worship, includes a significant emphasis on worldwide evangelism and care.

The 'Thousand Year's in the Bible

Following the above initial discussion on Millennialism, we continue this discussion with some additional views on Millennialism. Such a discussion will lead to a better understanding of the thousand years between Jesus' first coming into the world (His birth) and Jesus' second coming (His return) to the world. This discussion begins with verses taken from the Bible that speaks of thousand years, or of thousand hills.

The Thousand Years
Psalm 50:9-10,

> I have no need of a bull from your stall or of goats from your pens, for every animal of the forest is mine, and the cattle on a thousand hills.

Psalm 90:4,

For a thousand years in Yor sight are like a day that has just gone by, or like a watch in the night."

Ecclesiastes 6: 5, 6,

Though it (stillborn child 4) never saw the sun or knew anything, it has more rest than does that man—even if he lives a thousand years twice over but fails to enjoy this prosperity. Do not all go to the same place?

2 Peter 3:8,

But do not forget this one thing, dear friends: With the Lord a day is like a thousand years, and a thousand years are like a day. (Compare this with Ps. 90:4).

Revelation 20:2-3

He (angel) seized the dragon, that ancient serpent, who is the devil, or Satan, and bound him for a thousand years. He threw him into the Abyss, and locked and sealed it over him, to keep him from deceiving the nations anymore until the thousand years were ended. After that, he must be set free for a short time.

Revelation 20:4

I saw thrones on which were seated those who had been given authority to judge. And I saw the souls of those who had been beheaded because of their testimony for Jesus and because of the word of God. They had not worshiped the beast or his image and had not received his mark on their foreheads or their hands. They came to life and reigned with Christ a thousand years."

Revelation: 20:5-6,

The rest of the dead did not come to life until the thousand years were ended.) This is the first resurrection. Blessed and holy are those who have part in the first resurrection. The second death has no power over them, but they will be priests of God and of Christ and will reign with Him for a thousand years.

Revelation 20:7-8a,

When the thousand years are over, Satan will be released from his prison and will go out to deceive the nations in the four cor-ners of the earth—Gog and Magog—to gather them for battle.

An often-heard conclusion is that the time of "*thousand years*," used four times in Rev. 2-8, should not be taken literally, but used as a sym-bolic language, to indicate a long, undefined and undetermined period. That same period of a "*thousand years*" is also understood as literal 1000 years. Let us listen to two 'voices' who represent opposing perspectives of the '1000 years.'

Perspectives on the 'Thousand Years'
First, we will look at two opposing perspectives on the so called 'millen-nium' period presented by Harry R. Boer and Thomas D. Ice. These two perspectives will be followed by Stephen Whatley's overview 'Important Future Events.'

First Perspectieve
Harry Boer,[32] is very clear and direct on the 'thousand years' used in Rev. 20:1-10 as he explains as follows,

The millennium is pictured with a beginning and an end, but not a word is spoken about its nature, its content, the course of

---

[32] Harry R. Boer "*The Book of Revelation*,' More than 25 years a missionary teacher and theologian in Nigeria. Wm. B. Eerdmans Publishing Co. Grand Rapids, Michigan, 1979.

its history, or its purpose. Theological imagination has filled this period with all manner of activity, but it has done so without scriptural support... Revelation 20:1-10, with all its uncertainty, stands in a book that is more symbolic in character than in any other book in the Bible. (Pp. 132-133).

According to A-millennialism, the entire period from the first to the second coming of Christ is the millennium. Of it, the thousand years are a symbol.... Both, the Roman Catholic and the traditional Protestant churches hold to this view. A bit later, Boer writes that, in one way or another, there must be a millennium. In one way or another a whole dimension (of time, addition mine) must be added to history for which Scripture gives no support...Revelation does not know a Church that is at peace. (Pp. 135-137).

Harry Boer further explains that the Bible book Revelation knows only the Church as being under the cross of persecution...the suffering of the children of God is central...symbolized especially by the suffering of the martyrs...The martyr is the hero figure of Revelation. Not only that, the martyr of loyalty to Christ, of endurance, meekness, faithfulness, obedience and love is also the supreme symbol. This symbol, the martyr, John honours by picturing him as reigning in victory and peace for one thousand years. (Pp. 137-138).

Second Perspective
Thomas D. Ice,[33]

In the 'Thomas vs Hanegraaff' discussion, the latter says that the word "thousand" is rarely used in a literal sense throughout the Bible. Thomas agrees, saying "Outside of the six occurrences in Revelation 20, the term "a thousand years" is only used twice, Ps. 90:4 and 2 Pet. 3:8. In both instances, they require a literal use of a thousand years." However, even in these two cases one could argue that the use of the term 'thousand years' could be understood as an undefined but long period of time.

---

33 Thomas D. Ice, Perspective on *'ONE THOUSAND YEARS: LITERAL OR FIGURATIVE?'* Liberty University, May 2009, tdice@liberty.edu

Thomas includes a reference to the following perspective on the thousand years by Waymeyer who says:

> To be considered symbolic, the language in question must possess (a) some degree of absurdity when taken literally and (b) some degree of clarity when taken symbolically." (emphasis original) There is nothing absurd about taking a thousand years literally in Revelation 20, as was noted in the contextual uses of passages like Psalm 50:10–11. The literal reading of a 'thousand years' in Revelation 20 makes perfect sense. The only reason it may seem strange to an individual would be because they have a bias, for some reason, against such an understanding.
>
> Non-premillennialists seem to have just such a bias: if they let the statements of a thousand years stand, then this passage clearly teaches premillennialism. Waymeyer concludes, "it is difficult to imagine why one would consider the 'thousand years' in Revelation 20 to be symbolic language, for it possesses neither a degree of absurdity when taken literally, nor a degree of clarity when taken symbolically."[34]

The two above-described opposing perspectives on the meaning of the 'thousand years' mentioned in Rev. 20, are pointing out that this period, despite two different understandings for the 'thousand years,' makes it not easier to come to a clear-cut answer to what this period stands for in real time. One good reason to come to an acceptable conclusion can be drawn from what Waymeyer says, as mentioned earlier.

Before moving on to a next and third discussion we may go back to what Hanegraaff explained the thousand years in Revelation 20:1-7 in his book, THE APOCALYPSE CODE[35]. In footnote 72, p.256, he writes,

---

[34] Following is a much restrict overview of important future events in chronological order prepared by Stephen Whatley. In this overview the time period called Millennium is not inserted, as the author is looking into the future from an A-Millennium perspective.

[35] Hank Hanegraaff, *THE APOCALYPSE CODE*: Find out what the Bible really says about the end times and why it matters today, Nashville, Tennessee, 2007.

Failing to read Revelation in its appropriate historical and literary context, many have misconstrued John's words in Revelation 20 as a literary prophetic chronology according to which Satan will literally be bound for one thousand years, while the resurrected martyrs reign with Christ until the end of the "millennium," at which time the rest of the dead will be raised and Satan will be released to wage war against Christ and the resurrected saints. Rather than allowing one metaphorically rich passage in the apocalyptic letter of Revelation to override the rest of the clear passages in Scripture that teach a single, general resurrection of the dead (e.g., John 5:28-29; 1 Cor. 15:51-52; 1 Thess. 4:14-17), we must be willing to interpret this markedly symbolic passage in light of the rest of Scripture.

Whatley's Discussion on Sequential Future Events

Whatley's overview of important future events is based on an A-Millennium perspective, as he speaks of events beyond the so- called Millennium. From Jonathan Cahn's book, "*The Return of the gods*" I (Peter) understand that we are already beyond this Millennium period, he calls the Christian period This period is to be followed by today's Pre-Christian period beginning around 1965. This is my personal understanding as well.

Suggestion: As reader, you may be interested in listening to an interview with Jonathan Cahn: "Exposing Mysteries behind the Spiritual World – The State of America."

Overview of Sequential Future Events

1. The Conversion of all or many of the Jews, most of whom today are non-Christian (a common view of Rom. 11:1-32).
2. The Arrival of the Anti-Christ, when all unbelievers in the world will follow him vs. true believers (Rev. 13:1-10).
3. The Great Tribulation, which is led by the Anti-Christ vs. true believers (Rev. 13:5-10).
4. Christ's Second Coming (which occurs at the end of this age, followed by the age to come, i.e. Eternity (2 Pet. 3:10-13).

5. The Final Judgment of all: believers and unbelievers (Mt. 25:31-46; cf. also Lk. 17:20-37).

6. The Resurrection of all, with glorified bodies for the saved, first those who have died before His return, then those who are still alive at Jesus' return, (note addition mine) who never will die again (Jn. 5: 28-29 1 Cor. 15:42-43).

7. The New Heaven and New Earth (which only arrives at the beginning of the Eternal State (Rom. 4:13).

8. The New Jerusalem (Christian nation); all believers: Eternal antitype of the Canaan type (Rom. 4:13; Rev. 21—22).

[Note: Rev. 21:2 speaks of the Holy City, the new Jerusalem, as being the bride (Church) beautifully dressed for her husband, Jesus Christ, addition mine)].

In His resurrection and subsequent ascension at the end of His first Coming, Jesus began His rulership on the "throne of David"—from heaven and has been ruling over His people since then. He will rule from heaven until all of His unbelieving-enemies are subdued. Then He will return at His Second Coming to judge and to rule forever on the eternal, renewed earth and new heavens (cf. 1 Cor. 15:20-28; 2 Pet. 3:10-13; Rev. 11:15-18, and 21:1-5). This heavenly reign on "David's throne" is thus temporal, while Christ's reign on His throne is eternal: on the eternal new earth, new heaven, and new (restored) Jerusalem (2 Pet. 3:10-13; Rev. 11:15; 21:1-5).

Additional Discussion on Matters of Eschatology

Whatley understands the "1,000 year" reign-of-Christ scenario (Rev. 20:1-6) as a harmonization of the following factors:

(a) Christ rules one time temporally over the temporal earth from a temporal heaven on "David's throne" (Ac. 2:21-36; Rev. 20:1-6, interpreting the place as heaven: cf. Christ's "throne," the "souls," and "soul resurrection" in 12:5; 20:4; Eph. 2:1-6).

(b) Christ rules eternally over the eternal earth from the eternal earth on "David's throne" (Ps. 89:3-4, 34-37; Ezek. 37:24-28; Rev. 11:15-18; 21:1-5; 22:1-5).

(c) "1,000 years" to be interpreted as symbolic, i.e. "a long- time period," since the genre of the book of Revelation is apocalyptic, which means being written in a symbolic style (cf. Ps. 50:10).

According to Rev. 20, many texts show that Jesus' Second Coming will be followed by an eternal new heavens and earth, not by the Great Tribulation, as in Dispensationalism. The goal of God's covenantal dealings is, as it always has been, the gathering in and sanctifying of all [1] covenant people "from every nation, from all tribes ... peoples ... languages" (Rev. 7:9) [cf. the Abrahamic promise of a people]), who will one day inhabit the New Jerusalem in a renewed and lasting world order. (Read also Rev. 21:1-2).

In the New Covenant, the phrase "I will be your God, and you will be my People" includes many Gentiles who are added to (not replacing) the "faithful remnant" of Israel, therefore making an international people/church of faithful Jews and Gentiles in Christ (2 Cor. 6:14-16; 1 Pet. 2:9-10; Rev. 21:3, 9-14).

Rev. 20:7-9 is the Great Tribulation that follows the "Millennium," not a second Great Tribulation, as in Dispensationalism…There is only one Second coming of Christ and only one judgment, followed by eternity. That means that only one basis of judgment exists, which is whether one had a saving-faith in the promises of God regarding Christ, which is evidenced on earth by the fruit of works, such as loving our neighbors (Mt. 25:31-46; Jn. 5:24-29).

1 Thessalonians 4:13—5:11; 2 Thessalonians 1:6-10; 2:1-12 are the most detailed eschatology of Paul's entire teaching (cf. Jesus in this regard in Mt. 24—25). These Bible texts reveal nothing regarding the Millennium. In fact, 2 Thessalonians 1:6-10 does not allow millennialism from the time of Christ's Second Coming, especially a premillennial scenario, as all unbelievers will be "punished with everlasting destruction and shut out from the presence of the Lord" at the time of this Second coming. That means there will be no unbelievers for Christ to rule over on earth for 1,000 years, in any premillennial scheme…therefore, the Millennium must occur before Christ returns (Acts 2:29-36). That scenario fits His rule over His people from heaven -and- between His First and Second Coming (Acts 2:29-36).

There are two 'Comings' of Christ, namely the First Coming that initiates the New Covenant era, and then the Second Coming initiating the Eternal State. The Bible texts of 1 Thessalonians 4:13—5:11; 2 Thessalonians 1:6-10; 2:1-12 are the most detailed eschatology of Paul's entire teaching (cf. Jesus in this regard in Mt. 24—25), with all typical events included. Yet, they reveal nothing regarding the Millennium.

In fact, 2 Thessalonians 1:6-10 does not allow millennialism from the time of Christ's Second Coming, especially a premillennial scenario. Why? Because all unbelievers will be "punished with everlasting destruction and shut out from the presence of the Lord" at the time of this Second coming.

All this means, there will be no unbelievers for Christ to rule over on earth for 1,000 years, in any premillennial scheme, which means that the Millennium must occur before Christ returns (His one-and-only return). This time frame fits His rule over His people from heaven between His First and Second Coming (Acts 2:29-36). Hebrews 7:17-28; 8:1-13; 9:22-28; 10:1-18: Christ and His once-for-all-time sacrifice in the New Covenant, as the fulfillment of the Old Covenant sacrifices, forever ceases all animal sacrifices (even as "memorials").

God's Word speaks of Two Comings of Christ: First Coming initiates the New Covenant era, and the Second Coming (Return) initiating the Eternal State, as well as Two Ages: Present Age (since Christ's First Coming); Future Age (after Christ's Second Coming) that will be eternal.

There will be only one Second Coming of Christ and only one judgment, followed by eternity. That also means that there will be only one basis of judgment, namely whether one had saving-faith in the promises of God regarding Christ…Christ's return will lead to a new earth…as being completely and eternally victorious

(1 Cor. 15:20-26, 50-57; Rev. 11:135-18!)

Martyrdom and Persecution

In Floyd Brobbel's book[36] we read the following definition of being martyrs,

---

[36] Floyd A. Brobbel, *TROUBLE ON THE WAY*: PERSECUTION IN THE CHRISTIAN LIFE Genesis Publishing Group, Bartlesville., OK 74006, genesis-group.net

Martyrs are essentially those who willingly and faithfully follow Christ and refuse to allow threats of suffering, persecution, or death to stop them in their witness or misson....it requires a life wholly submitted to Christ, so that His glory will be revealed, whether that life lives or dies. Pp. 180-181. Then Brobbel also includes the following Bible words written by the apostle Paul,

"For to me to live is Christ, and to die is gain". Phil. 1:21.

The meaning of being a martyr is described as one who is experiencing different expressions of persecution due to holding on to a principle or cause, thereby sacrificing serious consequences, even death. Floyd Brobbel believes every Christian should know what persecution may lead to:

- The conditions, suffering, or death of a martyr [witness].
- Ridicule: To deride; make fun of; prepare for any form of persecution prepared the following overview of various forms of persecution entitled.
- Mockery: To annoy
- Harassment: To disturb; pester; trouble repeatedly
- Discrimination: To treat, or consider, or distinguish in favour of or against religious intolerance
- Defamation: To communicate false statements about a person that injure the reputation of that person
- Attack: To set upon in a forceful, violent, hostile, or aggressive way, with or without weapons
- Detainment: To seize, capture, or take or keep in custody by authority of law Torture: To inflict excruciating pain as punishment or revenge, as a means of getting a confession or information or subjection or sheer cruelty.

Martyrdom

The Bible has a lot to say about persecution, as Glen Penner[37] rightly points out that especially the New Testament was written by persecuted

---

[37] Glenn M. Penner, *In the Shadow of the Cross: A Biblical Theology of Persecution and Discipleship* (Bartlesville, OK: VOM Books, 204), 9.

believers to persecuted believers." The World Watch List,[38] developed by Open Doors, speaks of "institutionalized persecution," meaning that Christians are not on a level playing field with their non-Christian peers, despite having the education and skills that would make them eligible for such employment.

Following are examples to underscore the seriousness of persecution as described in several issues of The Epoch Times[39]

'Extremist views,'

A Christian law student, who supports the National Rifle Association (NRA), told The Epoch Times that he didn't know he'd been reported as "an extremist" for expressing conservative views until FBI agents knocked on his apartment door. They questioned him about his political views for more than an hour.

A journalism student said she felt bullied by a professor who forced students to parrot her scorn for America's "systemic racism" and affirm "progressive talking points" on immigration, gender-identity issues, "queer theory," intersectionality, transgenderism, religious faith, and the ideas of Karl Marx, author of "The Communist Manifesto.

I can't write what I truly believe" about these issues, Mia said, "When I did that, I got an F. To pass a class, I must affirm leftist ideas I don't believe in. When I repeat all the talking points and present them as ideas I believe wholeheartedly, I get As.

The Epoch Times[40] *'Are Universities Doomed?'*
Left-wing indoctrination; administrative bloat; obsessions with racial preferences; arcane, jargon-filled research; and campus-wide intolerance of diverse thought short-changed students, further alienated the public, and often enraged alumni.

---

[38] World Watch List, Open Doors <opendoorsusa.org/Christian-persecution/world-watch-list>.
[39] THE EPOCH TIMES, 'Students Speak Out on Anti-White, Anti-Christian, Anti-American Culture at Florida University', December 28, 2022.
[40] THE EPOCH TIMES, 'Are Universities Doomed?' by Victor Davis Hanson, December 22, 2022; updated December 27, 2022.

Persecution has been and will continue to be the hallmark of discipleship, as we understand Scripture,

"Consider it pure joy, my brothers, whenever you face trials of many kinds, because you know that the testing of your faith develops perseverance. Perseverance must finish its work so that you may be mature and complete, not lacking anything." (James 1:2-4).

Ten Ways to Pray for the Persecuted Church[41]

1. Pray that our persecuted brothers and sisters in Christ will sense God's presence. (Deut. 31:6; Ps. 34:17-18)
2. Pray they will feel connected to the greater body of Christ. (1 Cor. 12:20,26).
3. Pray they will experience God's comfort whenever family members are injured, imprisoned or even killed for their Christian witness. (2 Cor. 1:3-5).
4. Pray they will have the grace to love and forgive their persecutors. (Matt. 5:44).
5. Pray they will be protected and strengthened through the prayers of fellow believers around the world. (Hebr. 13:3; Ps. 34:7; Jude 20-25).
6. Pray their ministry activities will remain undetected by authorities or others who wish to silence them. Acts 9:25
7. Pray they will rejoice even amid suffering. (Acts 5:41).
8. Pray they will be refreshed through the study of God's Word, and thus encouraged to grow strong in their faith. (Eph. 6:17; Tim. 3:16-17).
9. Pray they will have more opportunities to share the Gospel. (Col. 4:4).
10. Pray for the boldness necessary to make Christ known, and for God's wisdom and direction as they endeavor to do so. (Phil. 1:14; James 1:5).

---

[41] The Voice of the Martyrs TEN WAYS To PRAY for the Persecuted Church, Special Edition: ANNUAL MINISTRY REPORT 2023.

Cahn's Prophetic Outlook on 2022
Excerpt of
An Interview of DAYSTAR with JONATHAN CAHN
January 12, 2022
(Please note that the following insights are still valuable in 2025)

Daystar: Over this last year we've seen more chaos and unrest overtake the world. Q. Why is it important that believers look to Biblical truth and the certainty of God's authority and faithfulness for comfort and encouragement in this year?

Cahn: God tells us that everything that can be shaken will be shaken. Thus, shaking is not necessarily a bad thing. It tells us what is sure and forever and what is not. When things are calm, we tend to get comfortable and rely on the world. But shaking has the effect of bringing us closer to God…. So, we must now anchor ourselves even more strongly to these spiritual truths as a ship anchors itself to a rock amid the waves.

Daystar: How important is prophecy regarding revealing God's purpose to His children on the Earth, and why should that give us boldness?

Cahn: We live in prophetic times, times in which the ancient prophecies of the Bible have come true before the eyes of the world, the return of the Jewish people to their ancient homeland, the rebirth of Israel, the restoration of Jerusalem. What prophecy tells us is that through it all and no matter what, God is still on the throne, His Word is true, His promises are faithful, and His love is everlasting. That should give us all the boldness we need to stand strong in the darkness and proclaim the truth to this generation.

Daystar: What has happened globally in 2021 that possibly lines up with Bible prophecy in your opinion?

Cahn: Most overtly, we've seen the continuation of what the Bible prophesies will happen in the last days--the great falling away or apostasy. We see it especially in America and the West, in nations that once stood on Biblical values, but are now not only departing from them, but overturning them, and warring against them…. The entire 'cancel culture' ultimately aims at cancelling the Bible and God's people. But this, too, is spoken in Biblical prophecy as reserved for the last days.

Cahn continues: There are growing signs warning us of the end of American pre-eminence as the head of nations. This too aligns with Biblical prophecy. In 2021 we saw the strengthening of alliances between Russia and both Iran and Turkey. These developments appear to align with Ezekiel 38 and 39. Last year saw also the increased opening up of the Temple Mount to Jewish people and even to Jewish prayer. At the same time, several breakthroughs were reported among those hoping to rebuild the Temple in Jerusalem, the restoration of the anointing oil, the red heifer, etc. [Peter: However, that building process will likely never be realized, as the Third Temple is to be understood as God's chosen people: the one final, everlasting Church].

Daystar: What message has God laid on your heart for believers in 2022 (2025)?

Cahn: The hour is late. If we are ever going to live as God called us to live, the time is now. If there's anything in our lives that shouldn't be there, the time is now, today, to begin getting it out. And if there's anything *not* in our lives that God has called us to be and do and rise to, the time is now, today, to begin rising to it. This we must do for our sake. But we must also do it for the world's sake, for America's sake. They need to see something real, something different, not like the world, but revolutionary. They need to see us living for real as the disciples of Messiah – as He called us to live.

Daystar: As more and more things happen that move us closer to the return of Jesus, how should believers be preparing their hearts and engaging the world right now?

Cahn: We need to remind ourselves that this is not our home. This is our mission field. We're not here to worry or live in fear--we're here to spread the Gospel and shine His light. And we need to remind ourselves that… the last word belongs to God. We are each bound for Heaven. While we're in this world, our job is to bring as many people as possible to get there with us.

Idol Worship in Today's Societies

The Return of the gods

Jonathan Cahn's book, "The Return of the gods," gives us a better understanding what has led to our very complex and anti-God kind of a world. Therefore, some of Cahn's insights are helpful in gaining a better understanding of the world we live in. Before looking at some conclusions from Cahn, we may first take note of the following recent comment[42] about the "modern moral compass,' directly followed by some Bible passages on worshipping idols of a 'pagan culture.'

The modern moral compass is rapidly shifting, creating a new standard of socially acceptable world views, and Christians are on the outside looking in. As intolerance grows in the ironic name of tolerance, believers must learn how to stand firm and reject the lies of the Devil.

Biblical Examples of a Pagan Culture

We may begin with looking at some Bible passages that speaks of a world in which we hear about worshipping idols in the following Bible verses:
Deuteronomy 32,

15 "Jeshurun grew fat and kicked; filled with food, he became heavy and sleek. He abandoned the God who made him and rejected the Rock his Savior. 16 They made him jealous with their foreign gods and angered him with their detestable idols. 17 They sacrificed to demons, which are not God—gods they had not known, gods that recently appeared, gods your fathers did not fear." (Deut. 32:15-17).

---

[42] The Friends of Israel Gospel Ministry, Pamphlet 'FEATURED RESOURCE,' Building bridges, Bringing hope. January, 2023.

Psalm 106,

36 "They worshiped their idols, which became a snare to them. 37 They sacrificed their sons and their daughters to demons. 38 They shed innocent blood, the blood of their sons and Daughters whom they sacrificed to the idols of Canaan, and the land was desecrated by their blood. They defiled themselves by what they did; by their deeds they prostituted themselves." (Ps. 106:36-38, Pp. 12, 13).

Matthew 12: The Sign of Jonah,

38 "Then some of the Pharisees and teachers of the law said to Him (Jesus), 'Teacher, we want to see a miraculous sign from you." 39 'He (Jesus) answered, '...43 "When an evil spirit comes out of a man, it goes through arid places seeking rest and does not find it. 44 Then it says, 'I will return to the house I left.' When it arrives, it finds the house unoccupied, swept clean and put in order. 45 Then it goes and takes with it seven other spirits more wicked than themselves, and they go in and live there. And the final condition of that man is worse than the first. That is how it will be with this wicked generation." (Matt. 12:38-45).

1 Corinthians 10,
In his first letter to the Corinthians Paul wrote the following words of warning concerning the differences between *Idol Feasts* and the Lord's Supper,

18 "Consider the people of Israel: Do not those who eat the sacrifices participate in the altar? 19 Do I mean then that sacrifice offered to an idol is anything, or that an idol is anything? 20 No, but the sacrifices of pagans are offered to demons, not to God, and I do not want you to be participants with demons. 21 You cannot drink the cup of the Lord and the cup of demons

too; you cannot have a part in both the Lord's Table and the table of demons." (1 Cor. 10:18-21).

Acts 16:

16 Once when we (Paul and Silas) were going to the place of prayer, we were met by a slave girl who had a spirit by which she predicted the future. She earned a great deal of money for her owners by fortune-telling. 17 This girl followed Paul and the rest of us, shouting, "These men are servants of the Most-High God, who are telling you the way to be saved."18 She kept this up for many days. Finally, Paul became so troubled that he turned around and said to the spirit, "In the name of Jesus Christ I command you to come out of her!" At that moment the spirit left her." (Ac. 16:16-18).

Spirits of Darkness and of Light

Spirits of Darkness are demonic spirits (demons) such as Jupiter, Apollo, Vesta and Bacchus are at war with the worship of God. Spirits of Light are angels, who are joined to the worship of God. p.13.

Please take note that these Bible texts show that references to evil spirits, demons and idols are not figments of one's imagination, but absolute, concrete realities at work in this present world we live in, and Jesus, as well as other authors of the Bible, relate to us.

Jonathan Cahn speaks of three different stages in world history, including pre-Christian, Christian and post-Christian civilizations. He then speaks of the differences between pre-and post-Christian societies as follows: (see also p.58)

A *pre*-Christian civilization may produce a Caligula or a Nero. But a *post*-Christian civilization will produce a Stalin or a Hitler.

A *pre*-Christian society may give birth to barbarity. But a *post*-Christian society will give birth to even darker offspring, Fascism, Communism, and Nazism.

A *pre*-Christian nation may erect an altar of human sacrifice. But a *post*-Christian nation will build Auschwitz.

We need to realize that between the *pre*-Christian and *post*-Christian societies we have the so-called Christian society. We may hereby think of the approx. 4000 years of the *pre*-Christian society as described in the Old Testament, then the Christian period beginning with the time described in the New Testament plus approx. the next 1950 years. That brings us to the third, *post*-Christian period that began around 1965.

This *post*-Christian began at the time that women in the Netherlands and Western Europe in general, became increasingly involved in all kinds of leadership positions, including pastoral positions. As a matter of fact, the first female pastor in the Netherlands began her pastoral ministry in the very village we lived in since our marriage.

The Possessor, The Enchantress, The Destroyer, The Transformer
Following those three different stages we read about three different gods: the Possessor, the Enchantress, the Destroyer, also described as The Dark Trinity. Then he speaks also of another god, the Transformer. Following is a brief overview of some responsibilities of those gods to get a better understanding of the time period we live in. We may listen to Cahn's following explanation in an interview he had and still can be seen on: *"Exposing Mysteries Behind the Spiritual World--The State of America."*

The Possessor.
This god helped America becoming increasingly alienated from God. The possessor was involved in changes made by the Supreme Court, as it had ruled against the display of the Ten Commandments and successively supported the president's action to enact laws and policies not supported by the ways of the Bible. Therefore, changes were made in the nation's public school system. With other changes the nation, as Cahn observed, became a *'civilization in spiritual schizophrenia.'*

That description of America was derived from other facts as well, such as changes made in the realms of morality, spirituality, politics, and culture. All this reflected the battle of Baal against God, thereby leading previous freedom and fulfillment into the bondage of the Baal. This change led to e.g. enslavement and bondage to/of pleasure, success, acceptance, sexual gratification, addictions, work, comfort, the internet, self-fulfillment, self-obsession.

The Enchantress

This female god (goddess), entitled *Queen of Heaven*, also known as Ishtar. She was the goddess of sexuality, whose worship was saturated with carnality, sensuality, and open sexuality. This led to the Sexual Revolution as a dimension of the paganization, as well as to the seduction of America and Western civilization. Under Ishtar, the goddess of instant gratification, sexuality was deified, and the severing of sexuality from marriage.

Through the present sex industry, we see the development of everything erotic: literature, dancing, massages, movies, as well as porn. Ishtar's so called dwelling place included sex, drugs and rock. So many more examples of Ishtar's influence, besides the sexual revolution, were also expressed in the overturning of gender, the weakening of the family, and the use of mind-altering substances.

The Destroyer

This third god of 'The Dark Trinity' is Molech. A refence to Molech is found in 1 Kings 11,

> On the hill east of Jerusalem, Solomon built a high place for Chemosh the detestable god of Moab, and for Molech the detestable god of the Ammonites. He did the same for all his foreign wives, who burned incense and offered sacrifices to their gods. (1 Kings 11:7-8).

Cahn continues by saying that Molech is associated with the sacrifice of children…with the sacrifice of children by their parents. Those grievous deeds are not only morally wrong and abhorrent but is thereby a sign of a nation that has turned away from God…Molech is the spirit and god of child sacrifice and thereby leads America away from God. In the late 1960s several American states legalized the killing of unborn children that eventually led the Supreme Court, on January 22, 1973, legalize the murder of unborn children, thereby opening the door for Molech to enter America.

Peter: Like it happened in pre-Christian Israel before, allowing their children to *"pass through the fire,"* it now happens in America that children are now also pierced, cut, torn apart, left to die, or, using chemical solutions—burned. America has its own Valley of Hinnom, allowing unwanted children being put to death. The blood of one million children had been spilled every year.

The Transformer

Ishtar, the female god, mentioned earlier as the goddess of sexuality, was also a sorceress. She embodied and personified ferocity, aggressiveness, violence, battle, war and destruction all characterizing her as a god with masculinity. Thus, we see Ishtar as being both a woman and a man. This goddess would seek to defeminize women, to masculinize them… thereby separate woman from man and man from woman to share in her nature. Consequently, women were now to be both their own protectors and defenders. Studies have revealed that since the beginning of the transformation those women had grown progressively unhappier.[43]

The Sign of the Rainbow Flag

This human-made design of the Rainbow Flag, in contrast to God's created Rainbow (Genesis 9), became the official symbol of gay pride. It has eight different colors representing eight different elements of the movement, presented in as many different colors under one unifying theme and common thread—the goddess Ishtar as she was the creator of the rainbow. The Rainbow flag consists of the following eight different colors,

> Pink: representing *sex*; Red: representing *life*; Orange: representing *healing*; Yellow: representing *light*; Green: representing *nature*; Turquoise: representing *magic*; Indigo: representing *serenity*; Violet: representing *spirit* (i.e. spirit of sexuality)

---

[43] Betsey Stevenson and Justin Wolfers, "The Paradox of Declining Female Happiness," Yale University, accessed May 26, 2022, https://law.yale.edu/sites/default/files/

The goddess Ishtar stretched herself across the sky, like a rainbow, to punish her offender. The rainbow becomes her mode of action and being, as behind its flowing colors was a banner of war. This approx. 40-year-old rainbow flag expresses the most powerful symbol of pride for the gay community, thereby saying, "This is who I am!" How that so-called rainbow differs from the original rainbow created by God!

The inspiration to the human made design of the approx. 40-year-old rainbow came from seeing the original rainbow in the sky, created by its original Designer, the Almighty God, Maker of the heavens and earth. We read about the original rainbow as a covenant sign the following words in the Bible book Genesis, Chapter 9: 8-15a,

> I (God, addition mine) now establish My covenant with you (Noah, addition mine): Never again will all life be cut off by waters of a flood; never again will there be a flood or destroy the earth. And God said, "This is the sign of the covenant I am making between Me and you and every living creature with you, a covenant of all generations to come: I have set my rainbow in the clouds, and it will be the sign of the covenant between Me and the earth. Whenever I bring clouds over the earth and the rainbow appears in the clouds, I will remember My covenant between Me and you and all living creatures of every kind.

The human-made rainbow as the official symbol of pride for the gay community is an ugly copy of the design of the actual rainbow we see in the sky, created by God as a covenant sign for His people. What a contrast!

Signs of the Post-Christian Era

We need to return to what Jonathan Cahn wrote in his book, "The Return of the gods," in which he gives us a better understanding of what has led to our very complex, anti-God kind of world in which we hear increasingly about symptoms of a growing spiritual crisis of worshipping idols belonging to a growing 'pagan culture.' Cahn reminds us of the following three different stages in world history: the pre-Christian, Christian and post-Christian civilizations.

Earlier on, p. 163, we were reminded of the approx. 4000 years of a *pre*-Christian society in the Old Testament, followed by a Christian period of about 1960 years, beginning with the time of the New Testament. It was then mentioned that the third, *post*-Christian period, began about the beginning around 1965.

In case someone may suggest that the so-called period of 'thousand years,' as an undefined period, could refer to the Christian period, I (Peter) will say a few things about this Christian period on pages 170-171.

Europe: A Physical and Spiritual Battlefield

The Christian period has seen Satan's influence in creating spiritual and physical conflicts between the Catholic Church (Rome) and the Protestant Church. The Crusades were a series of religious wars initiated, supported, and sometimes directed mainly by the Roman Catholic Church during the period 1095-1291.

Those crusades were in fact military expeditions to the land of Israel in the Middle East to prevent that, especially Jerusalem, would come under the rule of Muslims. Especially the conquest of Jerusalem in 1099 stands out among the many military campaigns that have taken place in those years, though outside Europe. (One may read my book, *THE REAL DEAL: Making the Case for the One True God*; *Implications for Radical Islam and the Global Church.*

Those many years of warfare by thousands of Europeans was followed by the so-called Pre-Reformation period with John Wycliffe (1328-1884) in England and in Germany as well, and of John Huss (1373) in Prague.[44] Both brothers in the Lord caused tumultuous times to say the least. As a matter of fact, they became forerunners of an even greater tumultuous time, including the centuries-long spiritual struggle, a period of many persecutions. That period was called the period of the Reformation, beginning with Martin Luther in the early AD 1400, followed by Zwingli (Switzerland) and Calvin (France).

---

[44] Williston Walker, *A HISTORY OF THE CHRISTIAN CHURCH*, Charles Scribner's Sons, New York, 1970

During the pre-Reformation and the actual Reformation periods, thousands of reformers (Christians) were killed, most often by public crucifixions. One such public crucifixion, also referred to as the martyr's pile, happened in Paris,

> There was no pulpit like the martyr's pile. The serene joy that lighted up the faces of these men as they passed along…to the place of execution, their heroism as they stood amid the bitter flames, their meek forgiveness of injuries, transformed, in instances not a few, anger into pity, and hate into love, and pleaded with resistless eloquence on behalf of the gospel.[45]

Then again, later, referring to the league contemplated by the reformed princes, Luther declared that the only weapon employed in this warfare should be "the sword of the Spirit,"

> …From the secret place of prayer came the power that shook the world in the Great Reformation.[46]
> The Protestant Reformers have built on Christ, and the gates of hell could not prevail against them.[47]

Add to those Reformation Periods the two World Wars WW I: 1914-1918 and WW II: 1939-1945, we can reasonably assume that the Christian period has seen serious wars and upheavals, as we thereby think of the many crusades made by Europeans to the Middle East during the period to face the radical Muslims who fought on behalf their god, Allah. One thing we learn from that so called second, Christian period is that the often called "thousand years of peace and prosperity" has no reference to the two thousand years of various wars in Europe with Satan operating reasonably freely.

---

[45] E. G. White, *THE GREAT CONTROVERSY*, Celebrating the 500th Anniversary, Remnant Publication, Inc., 2017.

[46] E. G. White, *THE GREAT CONTROVERSY*, Celebrating the 500th Anniversary, Remnant Publication, Inc., 2017, 132.

[47] Ibid. p. 133.

With this Christian period in Europe behind us, we are then reminded by Cahn of the beginning of a new period, including North America, with the return of the **Dark Trinity** including three different gods: the Possessor, the Enchantress, the Destroyer. I believe that this period, described in the Old Testament, leads us towards and into the so-called end times.' This third and final period in world history also led, and continues to lead, Jewish people from all over the world back to their God-given land in the Middle East: Israel since 1948.

In our present post-Christian era, with the Dark Trinity of the pre-Christian era in place, and operating again in the Western world, we understand that Satan seems to have regained his presence and the reality of persecution, i.e. the undermining of well-functioning societies. We are presently experiencing a dis-integration of the Western World, while the previous Christian influence in societies is being undermined and slowly but surely mitigated. Christianity is maneuvered into the 'backseat' of society, thereby providing the opportunity for Satan moving towards the front seat.

It seems appropriate to listen to the answer Perry Stones once gave to his own question,

> Q: In the Bible, the Antichrist is referred to as the lawless one, so is the current rejection of truth a sign that we're seeing increasingly the influence of an antichrist-spirit.

> A: 2 Thessalonians, Chapter 2, is one of the most important New Testament chapters exposing the spirit of lawlessness that is unleashed, leading mankind to the final great deception. Paul wrote that people would fall into the satanic trap of deception because, They received not the love of the truth" (2 Thess. 2:10), as they, "Believed not the truth." (2 Thess. 2:12).

Such a rejection of truth is the culprit of deception during the end times. Paul warned that in the end times, people would give themselves to, "Seducing spirits and doctrines of devils"

(1 Tim. 4:1). Being seduced means being drawn away from something to the point of becoming someone who is roving around without direction. In context, Paul is alluding to people who are drawn away (seduced) from solid doctrine. However, we must abide in truth, be truth-lovers and truth-seekers. The truth will *live*, will sets us *free*, while the lie will *die*.

Articles of The Epoch Times

The Epoch Times, February 11, 2023

Americans Tell CEOs: Drop the 'Woke' and Get Back to Business. New survey finds bipartisan majority are more likely to buy from companies that are politically neutral. As companies gear up for an economic downturn, cutting costs and staff, CEOs might want to heed the rising voice of consumers who want them to focus on business rather than on politics.

According to a recent poll of more than 1,000 likely voters by the Trafalgar Group and Convention of States Action (COSA), nearly 80 percent said that, given the choice, they are more likely to buy from a company that is politically neutral. In a rare case of bipartisan consensus, both Democrats (76.9 percent) and Republicans (78.8 percent) felt this way in roughly equal measure.

Mark Meckler, COSA president, told The Epoch Times that the message to CEOs was: "Go back to doing what you were hired to do, which is to make money for shareholders."

"This is a blowback that's coming," Meckler said. "It's coming big time against all this 'woke' politics in business. It's not even that folks want their companies to reflect their politics; they want their companies, the people they buy from, to just ignore politics."

The term "woke" is used by both liberals and conservatives to describe several more radical progressive ideologies, including critical race theory, social justice, and gender theory.

The Epoch Times, July 14, 1923

In its article, "Why Societies go mad" reference was made to the book 'Political Ponerology' describing how Governments become Evil.

Ponerology is The Science of Evil, Psychopathy, and the Origins of Totalitarianism, a book written by Andrew M. Lobaczewski. Political Ponerology is shocking in its clinically descriptions of the true nature of evil. It is poignant in its more literary passages revealing the immense suffering experienced by the researchers contaminated or destroyed by the disease they were studying.

Political Ponerology is a study of the founders and supporters of oppressive political regimes. Lobaczewski's approach analyzes the common factors that lead to the propagation of man's inhumanity to man. Morality and humanism cannot long withstand the predations of this evil. Knowledge of its nature and its insidious effect on both individuals and groups - is the only antidote.

The reason for bringing attention to this book is that it addresses the problems we are facing these days in North America. It explains why our Far left/Radical liberal governments are interpreting the social-political perspectives of Karl Marx and Friedrich Engels. We are speaking here about the Psychology of Evil, the origin of totalitarianism.

You may consider reading my previous book, *THE RIGHT DEAL: Making the Case for a More Respectful Society.*

(Note: My author's name: Rev. Peter Hendriks Okello).

CHAPTER FIVE
END-TIME DEVELOPMEMTS

Speaking of developments during the so-called 'end-time' period, many would not expect that the Old Testament has anything meaningful to say about such a time. However, one OT prophet, Daniel, has something to share with us about end-time developments. What he must share with us seems worthy looking at, if not taken seriously, as they seem to make sense to us living in, what many consider to be the end-times.

Daniel, Chapter Seven
So, let us turn to the Bible book Daniel, Chapter 7, with the heading, "Daniel's Dream of the Four Beasts." We will look at verses that attract our attention, as they seem to refer to previous and recent developments concerning future developments. I (Peter) take hereby the liberty to make either abbreviations of the text, or writing the complete verses Daniel saw and heard in a dream:

> 2 In my vision I saw the four winds of heaven churning up the great sea. 3 Four great beasts, each different from the others, came up out of the sea. ...4-7 First beast was like a lion... second beast looks like a bear...third beast looks like a leopard with four wings and four heads...and the fourth beast, terrifying and frightening and very powerful, having iron teeth—crushing and devouring its victims...having ten horns...8 Then, another horn, came up among those horns; and three of the first horns were uprooted before it, a little one with eyes like

a man, and a mouth that spoke boastfully…11 The (fourth) beast was slain, its body destroyed and thrown into the blazing fire, 12 the other beasts had been stripped of their authority, but were allowed to live for a period of time." 17-18 In these two verses we read that those four beasts are actually four kingdoms that will arise from the earth. But the saints of the Most-High will receive the (one) Kingdom and will possess it forever. (Dan. 7: 2-12, 17-18).

Note: These last two sentences have eschatological significance, as the Kingdom refers to the everlasting kingdom.

19 Then David wanted to know the true meaning of especially the fourth beast, as it was different from the other beast, as well as most terrifying 20 and the meaning of the 10 horns, its head, as well as the other horns that came up. 21 This last horn was waging war against the saints and defeating them. 22 Then the Ancient of days pronounced judgment in favor of the saints of the Most-High, and in due time possessed the kingdom.

23, 24 The Most High gave the following explanation:

The Fourth beast is a fourth kingdom, being different from all other kingdoms…devouring the whole earth. Ten horns are ten kingdoms coming from that kingdom devouring the whole earth. Then another king will arise, different from the earlier ones, subduing three kings. 25 This last king will speak against the Most-High and oppress the saints and try to change the set times and laws. The saints will be handed over to him for a time, times and a half a time.

26 Then the court will sit, and his power will be destroyed forever. 27 Then the sovereignty, power and greatness of the kingdoms under the whole heaven will be handed over to the saints, the people of the Most-High. His kingdom will be an

everlasting kingdom, and all rulers will worship and obey him. 28a This is the end of the matter.

We may now also turn to Daniel 12: The End Times.

1 At that time Michael, the great prince who protects your people, will arise. There will be a time of distress such as has not happened from the beginning of nations until then. But at that time your people—everyone whose name is found written in the book—will be delivered. 2 Multitudes who sleep in the dust of the earth will awake: some to everlasting life, others to shame and everlasting contempt. 3 Those who are wise will shine like the brightness of the heavens, and those who lead many to righteousness, like the stars for ever and ever. (Dan. 12:1-3).

Following Daniel's visions of future end time developments, we may turn to Bible verses that also speak of future developments during the so-called end-time period. The Bible verses below are taken from the Old and New Testaments, as they seem to relate and eventually leading up, to Armageddon's climactic battle (more on that in Chapter Six) in world history.

[Note that the Antichrist is also described as a 'beast of a man,' also referred to as a 'dangerous monster', having received power from Satan].

Biblical References
Luke 21: Signs of the End of the Age. In this Bible chapter, Jesus is responding to His disciples who were speaking to Him as they marveled about the temple's beautiful stones and gifs dedicated to God:

6 "As for what you see here, the time will come when not one stone will be left on another; every one of them will be thrown down." 7 "Teacher," they asked, "when will these things happen? And what will be the sign that they are about to take place?" 8 He replied: "Watch out that you are not deceived. For many will come in My name, claiming, "I am he,' and 'The

time is near.' Do not follow them. 9 When you hear of wars and revolutions, do not be frightened. These things must happen first, but the end will not come right away." 10 Then He said to them: "Nation will rise against nation, and kingdom against kingdom. 11 There will be great earthquakes, famines and pestilences in various places, and fearful events and great signs from heaven." (Lk. 21:6-11).

Note: See also Matthew 24:3-8.
Thessalonians 2: The Man of Lawlessness (Antichrist)

1 "Concerning the coming of the Lord Jesus Christ and our being gathered to Him...3 that day will not come, until the rebellion occurs, and the man of lawlessness is revealed, the man doomed to destruction. 4 He will oppose and will exalt himself over everything that is called God or is worshiped, so that he sets himself up in God's temple, proclaiming himself to be God....

9 "The coming of the lawless one will be in accordance with the work of Satan displayed in all kinds of counterfeit miracles, signs and wonders, 10 and in every sort of evil that deceives those who are perishing. They perish because they refused to love the truth and so be saved." 2 Thess.2:1, 3, 4, 9-10.

1 Timothy 4: Instructions to Timothy

1 The Spirit clearly says that in later times some will abandon the faith and follow deceiving spirits and things taught by demons. 2 Such teachings come through hypocritical liars, whose consciences have been seared as with a hot iron." (1 Tim. 4:1-2).

2 Timothy 4: Paul is charging Timothy

1 I give you this charge: 2 Preach the Word; be prepared in season and out of season; correct, rebuke and encourage with great

patience and careful instruction. 3 For the time will come when men will not put up with sound doctrine. Instead, to suit their own desires, they will gather around them a great number of teachers to say what their itching ears want to hear. 4 They will their ears away from the truth and turn aside to myths. 5 But you, keep your head in all situations, endure hardship, do the work of an evangelist, discharge all the duties of your ministry. (2 Tim. 4:1-5).

Reflecting on especially vs. 3 of the above passage, we may agree that in our days we are living in the 'post-Christian' in which many don't put up with sound doctrines. That is not only true concerning our societies, but also in a growing number of local churches as well, as I have noticed in our local church.

Revelation 16: The Seven Bowls of God's Wrath

This Chapter Five, we read about seven angels and each of them pouring out a bowl expressing God's Wrath in the following different ways as follows:

2 "The first angel went and poured out his bowl on the   land, and ugly and painful sores broke out on the people   who had the mark of the beast and worshiped his image, 3 The second angel poured out his bowl on the sea, and it turned into blood like that of dead man, and everything living thing in the sea died, 4 The third angel poured out his bowl on the rivers and springs of water, and they became blood....

8 The fourth angel poured his bowl on the sun, and the sun was given power to scorch people with fire. 9 They were by the intense heat, and they cursed the name of God, who had control over these plagues, but they refused to repent and glorify Him. 10 The fifth angel poured out his bowl on the throne of the beast, and his kingdom plunged into darkness. Men gnawed their tongues in agony 11 and cursed the God of heaven because of their pains and their sores, but they refused to repent of what they had done. 12 The sixth angel poured his

bowl on the great river Euphrates, and its water was dried up to prepare the way for the kings from the East.

13 Then I saw three evil spirits that looked like frogs; they came out of the mouth of the dragon, and out of the mouth of the beast and out of the mouth of the false prophet. 14 They are spirits of demons performing miraculous signs, and they go out to the kings of the whole world, to gather them for the battle on the great day of God Almighty. 15 "Behold, I come like a thief! Blessed is he who stays awake and keep his clothes with him, so that he may not go naked and be shamefully exposed." 16 Then they gathered the kings together to the place that in Hebrew is called Armageddon. 17 The seventh angel poured out his bowl into the air, and out of the temple came a loud voice from the throne, saying "It is done!"

18 Then there came flashes of lightning, rumblings, peals of thunder and a severe earthquake. No earthquake like it has ever occurred since man has been on earth, so tremendous was the quake. 19 The great city split into three parts, and the cities of the nations collapsed. God remembered Babylon the Great and gave her the cup filled with the wine of the fury of His wrath. 20 Every island fled away, and the mountains could not be found. 21 From the sky huge hailstones of about a hundred pounds each fell upon men. And they cursed God on account of the plague of hail. Because the plague was so terrible. (Rev.16:1-21).

Signs of the Anti-Christian Era

Revelation 13: The Beast is understood to be the Antichrist

There seems to be a growing public interest in who the Antichrist is. Google informs us that more than 183 million hits ask who this Antichrist is. Skip Heitzig helps us understand that Revelation 13 speaks of "The Beast out of the Sea, (vss. 1-10), as well as the Beast out of the Earth (vss. 11-18). Notice the last verse, vs. 18, "This calls for wisdom.

If anyone has insight, let him calculate the number of the beast, for it is man's number. His number is **666**." (Rev. 13:1-18).

The number **666** points out the Antichrist: Satan, also called the Man of Lawlessness we read about in 2 Thessalonians 2:1-12. He will have the power of persuasion, such as Hitler had prior to and during WWII. One may then also read Mathew 24 that speaks of the 'End of this Age. Especially Matt. 24:15, that leads us back to the O.T. Book Daniel, Chapters 7, 8, 9, 11, 12.

Present articles also point to the coming, if not already, difficult times that could conceivably lead to the predicted Antichrist. It seems that signs of living in or living towards an anti-Christian era it especially expressed in the arena of present-day politics, as well as in social and moral behaviours, as we will take note of.

Articles from The Epoch Times

The following article by THE EPOCH TIMES may be seen as initial signs and impressions of the coming (or the already) Antichristian Era. This is an independent newspaper with the goal of restoring accuracy and integrity in the media and receives much interest among readers.

Following is an article entitled: **A Global 'Emergency Platform' Could Be the UN's Next Tool to Establish Global Tyranny.**

By Augusto Zimmermann, July 26, 2023

In September 2024, the U.N. General Assembly will be hosting "The Summit of the Future," where member states will be invited to adopt an agreement that further consolidates globalist policy reforms offered over the past two years, including the notorious U.N. 2030 Agenda and the Paris Climate Agreement. "Our Common Agenda" is the United Nations' vision for strengthening global governance for present and future generations."

Many radical proposals are contained in that important document, but the most important proposal seems to be the plan for a new "emergency platform" to respond to "complex global shocks." "A complex global shock" is vaguely described in this document as "an event with severely disruptive consequences for a significant proportion of the global population that leads to secondary impacts across multiple sectors."

That basically means that the U.N. secretary-general would receive extraordinary powers that are, in principle, devoid of any legal-institutional limits, all without authorisation from the member states to an emergency platform in place, indefinitely.

The late Austrian-British economist and philosopher Friedrich Hayek, a Nobel Prize laureate, once offered this sobering reflection about the unending use of emergency powers:

"Emergencies' have always been the pretext on which the safeguards of individual liberty have been eroded—and once they are suspended; it is not difficult for anyone who has assumed such emergency powers to see to it that the emergency will persist."

To conclude, the implementation of the emergency platform would constitute the biggest step towards the establishment of a global tyranny based on the principles of international socialism. This would confer to a few individuals the extraordinary power to exercise absolute control over the lives of every person living in this world. Above all, if the use of the "emergency platform" by the U.N. secretary-general becomes a reality, the world as we know will cease to exist. We either stand for our basic rights and freedoms, or risk losing everything on October 2024. (Note: this has not happened yet – (March 5, 2025).

An article like the one just quoted on previous page, could be interpreted as a step that, overtime, could eventually lead to the rise of the predicted Antichrist. Regarding such a possible development, one may listen carefully to an article by Kevin Stocklin: Biden Admin Negotiates Deal to Give WHO Authority Over US Pandemic Policies. That article reads:

The Biden administration is preparing to sign up the United States to a "legally binding" accord with the World Health Organization (WHO) that would give this Geneva-based UN subsidiary the authority to dictate America's policies during a pandemic.

However, most recently, January 20, 2025, we read that President Trump is making good on his preelection pledge to withdraw from the

World Health Organization. In one of many orders issued after his recent inauguration, he announced the start of the process for terminating U.S. membership in the U.N. agency that oversees global health issues.

Trump's frustration with WHO goes back to the height of the COVID era. He's repeatedly criticized the organization for being too slow to respond to the pandemic and being "owned and controlled by China." (Fr. 'Get the Goats and Soda newsletter')

The Epoch Times Sep. 18, 2023
  Viewpoint by James Corrie
  Subject: Global Governance Is (Almost) Here
  Europe leads the drive for worldwide issuance of digital IDs, vaccine passports, and centralized control of AI… There's a grand movement afoot known by different titles at the United Nations, but it generally falls under the Agenda 2030 rubric, which will change the world and eliminate our rights as Americans without so much as a whimper of dissent from our federal government.

The Deconstruction of the Nation-State

This apparent deconstruction of the United States and the nation-state, in general, is part of a larger and sustained scheme by the U.N. and other transnational and global institutions, such as the European Union and the World Health Organization (WHO), to shift the national power and policies of all nations on Earth, no matter what the domestics resistance may be, up to the supranational or global governance level.

In response to some of the above articles we read: Another step toward a worldwide Antichrist, if the above articles could be a sign if they could signify whether we are moving to, or already experiencing, the realty of the predicted coming of the Antichrist. The above-mentioned articles could be interpreted as radical political changes towards the time that we have indeed the rise of the actual Antichrist figure.

The Realm of Social and Moral Behaviors

Another sign of living in an increasingly anti-Christian era can be distracted from the following articles by The Epoch Times, Mar. 28, 2023,

Douglas Burton: Children Groomed for Trans Lifestyle by Gender Ideology in Schools: Excerpts:

Parents protest outside the Davis Joint Unified School District offices over a talk featuring Rachel Pepper, co-author of "The Transgender Child," in Davis, Calif., on Jan. 11, 2023. On March 23, a public forum in Eldersburg, Maryland, heard from a panel of experts that public schools are grooming vulnerable students to transition away from their sex at birth. Maryland parents are on the warpath against gender ideology, which they believe is steering their County Superintendent of Schools to notify a parent when his or her child signals a desire to change gender. The gathering was sponsored by Moms for Liberty and co-sponsored by the Heritage Foundation and the Leadership Institute.

"Public school teachers are socially transitioning students because they think they are being kind," said Kathleen Goonan, a retired medical doctor who spends her time now helping de-transitioners, young people who have previously transitioned and who now want to reverse the process under medical care. "The fact is that social transitioning is a major psycho-social intervention, in which teachers are fast-tracking kids toward medical change," said Goonan. Advocates such as Goonan must tread lightly, since 21 states and the District of Columbia have passed laws banning "conversion therapy," a treatment in which a physician assists a person who is seeking to revert to his or her sexual identity at birth.

A physician doing so could suffer the loss of their medical license. The Biden administration has made gender identity a protected class," Dr. Ryan Anderson told the forum. "It means that a doctor could be delicensed for helping a child become comfortable with his or her body, said Anderson, who is the author of the book "When Harry Became Sally" (2017).

The Epoch Times April 13-19, 2023
Sex-Change bans for Minors Surge in Conservative US States with 12 states ban sex changes for minors; 19 more have ongoing legislation.

The Epoch Times November 2-8, 2023
Example of present-time social behavior by Jeffrey A. Tucker who listened to the founder and owner of a very successful accountancy firm, telling him that she could not find competent workers,

> They might have credentials, but they cannot finish tasks. They lack professional scrupulosity, much less real pride in what they do. They slog to the office when convenient and look for every excuse not to be there. They take every hour of paid time off and use every sick day.

In the same article Tucker also shares with his readers the following personal observation,

> Another thing is just how entitled people under 35 years of age are. Everything in the office has to be just right, not just the temperature in the room but the coffee, the chair, the positioning of the window, all colleagues, and so on. They are just looking for excuses to complain…What an environment!

The above two excerpts were written in an article under the headline: Can Demoralized and Lazy People Fight for Liberty?

True Christians could become Endangered Species
From an ADF International email on September 19, 2023, we learned that "Imperialism of so-called "woke culture" – which seems to be growing by the day in its anti-Christian ideologies – is threatening freedom worldwide. As an example, it says that,

In the West, governments increasingly are trying to silence and punish speech they deem unacceptable by law think of "Hate speech" or censorship zone laws.

At the same time, ADF International also admits that,

In a free society, ideas should be challenged with ideas, not criminal penalties.

Such a challenge has become apparent in a recent decision of the European Court of Human Rights concerning the right to free expression, as the Supreme Court in the United States chose freedom over fear.

While that being true, I believe in the future, we, as staunch followers of Christ, may expect challenges and opposition even within local churches and various denominations.

Sudden War in the Middle East

Nearly one-and-a half years ago, the world was shocked by the unexpected, horrible attack of Hamas on Israel on Oct. 7, 2023.

Without going into detail about that event and subsequent events following that inhuman, evil-filled event, some voices were predicting the possibility of a coming Armageddon in the near future. One may read what the Jewish Holocaust survivor Gabor Mate said regarding this war.[48]

By the time you read this book, that horrible situation has already develop into Lebanon in October 2024, defeating Hezbollah. This war could eventually develop into a war with Iran. At the time you read this book this war has stopped early 2025 due to ongoing discussions to end this war. It did end during January 2025, at a time that Donald Trump became President of America for a second time on January 20.

I personally believe in the possibility that the next 4 years could become a rather peaceful period in the Middle East, as long as Trump remains President, as he is very supportive of Israel. At the same time,

---

48 One also may watch the video on Facebook https://fb.watch/nSuZXnTE31/?mibex-tid=j8LeHn.or www.facebook. com

those coming 4 years could be used by Muslim groups, such as Hamas and Hezbollah, to build up and strengthen their military capacity to attack Israel again with the help of surrounding Muslim countries.

We should not be surprized that, following the 4-year period with Trump as President, that with a possible and somewhat 'weaker' American President, a renewed and much stronger Muslim attack on Israel will occur. In such a case, we may wonder if we could speak of the possible reality of that future and long-expected Armageddon between Israel and surrounding Muslim world.

See Chapter Six.

For those interested in the history of the Israelites related to their God-given land, are reminded of a much earlier and similar story in the Bible:

How God sent the Israelites from Egypt into the land He had chosen for His covenant, though also rebellious, people. We read in the Bible book Joshua how Joshua let the Israelites into their promised land thereby crossing the Jordan and then had to fight the Canaanites, Hittites, Hivites, Perizzites, Girgashites, Amorites and Jebusites (Joshua 3:9-10).

Since then, the Israelites have been involved in many wars mentioned the Old Testament and beyond. The story about Israel throughout history demonstrates that there has been no people in this world other than Israel that has suffered so much. One may read Ezekiel 39: 25-29, as well as see a video named:

Israel at war: What do the Hamas attacks on Israel mean for End times prophesy. Skip Heitzig.

Antichrist's True Identity
Let us briefly return to Thessalonians 2: The Man of Lawlessness, where we read,

> The coming of the lawless one will be in accordance with the work of Satan displayed in all kinds of counterfeit miracles, signs and wonders....and will, 4b set himself up in God's temple...proclaiming himself to be God. (Thess. 2: 9, 4b).

Earlier on, it has been clarified that the so-called Antichrist will at some point in time enter the Third Temple. It was also understood that this Third Temple has been identified as God's chosen people, the final Church. In that case, we need to identify the one who is going to enter the Church, being God's chosen people.

So far, we have not heard who will enter God's chosen people, since the Antichrist is not a person. That leaves us with the possibility that the identity of the Antichrist could well be Satan, who not only will, but already has entered the lives of many people...

As we realize that mankind had entered the dominion of Satan, namely the earth, as Jesus testified that He had seen Satan fallen from heaven to earth (Luke 10:18), then still empty. Failing to replace God, Satan had only one thing in mind, namely, to drive generations of people away from God, beginning with Adam and Eve. He has shown to be very successful in doing so during all successive generations of people up to this day. His most interest is to also draw Christians away from God, from the Lord Jesus Christ. He has been, so far, successful in such an attempt. It is only by holding on to Jesus as his or her Savior that a Christian wants and is able to resist and reject Satan through the encouragement and power of the Holy Spirit!

In Revelation 22:15 we hear Jesus prompting His followers not to get involved in immoral activities. The Antichrist, Satan, is the pusher of immoral behavior on a large scale, including Christians. As a result, many local churches see members leaving local churches that accept those living in homosexual relationships. For that reason, and other reasons, many churches that have already closed their doors, and more could follow.

CHAPTER SIX

THE CLIMATIC BATTLE OF ARMAGEDDON

Crescendo concerning the End Times
Psalm of David

"Those who hate me without reason outnumber the hairs of my head; many are my enemies without cause, those who seek to destroy me. I am forced to restore what I did not steal." (Ps. 69:4).

Armageddon: Location, Meaning, History

Armageddon is one of the richest agricultural areas of the state of Israel and is often called Israel's breadbasket. It runs from the Bay of Haifa on the northern coast in a southeast direction to the River Jordan. It is fifteen miles wide at its greatest breadth, the valley of Esdraelon (its Greek name is still used today) is flanked on the north by the Nazareth ridge and on the south by Mount Carmel, Mount Gilboa, and the hills of Samaria, located some sixty miles north of Jerusalem. Today, the Jews use this area, called the Kidron Valley, as a burial ground.

This area is situated on the flank of a hill, known as *Har-Megiddo* or the "Mount of Megiddo," translated 'the place of troops." The word *Armageddon* is often used in reference to any type of catastrophic conflict, especially if it's seen as likely to result in widespread destruction or the annihilation of human life. In the Bible the word *Armageddon* refers to a climactic future battle between God and the forces of evil.

See Revelation 16:1-21: The Seven Bowls of God's Wrath, as described earlier in Chapter Five.

Throughout history, armies have fought countless battles in that region: Egyptians, Assyrians, Greeks, Romans, and Crusaders fought in Megiddo, as well as the armies of Napoleon. This so called 'greatest natural battlefield in the world' has been used as the site of battles during World War I and the Arab-Israeli War of 1948. Before that time, the plain of Megiddo, or Armageddon, was famous for two great victories in Israel's history: 1) Barak's victory over the Canaanites (Judges 4:15) and 2) Gideon's victory over the Midianites (Judges 7). Armageddon was also the site of two great tragedies:

1) the death of Saul and his sons (1 Samuel 31:8) and

2) the death of King Josiah (2 Kings 23:29–30; 2 Chron. 35:22).

Concerning the future: a final and decisive battle will take place as mentioned in Revelation 19:11–20. That final battle will take place sometime in the future, and will eventually end by divine intervention, thereby defeating the forces of the Antichrist. Those forces could well be of Muslim or Islamic origin, as was the case with the well-known October 7 war.

In Revelation 16, we read what led to the final, terrible Battle of Armageddon as we turn to verse 12 that speaks of the sixth angel as follows,

12 "The sixth angel poured out his bowl on the great river Euphrates, and its water was dried up to prepare the way for the kings from the East. 13 Then I saw three evil spirits that looked like frogs: out of the mouth of the beast and out of the mouth of the false prophet. 14 They are spirits of demons performing miraculous signs, and they go out to the kings of the whole world, to gather them for the battle on the great day of the God Almighty. (Rev. 16:12-14).

Considering those three evil spirits, mentioned above and referred to as *'spirits of demons performing miraculous signs, and they go out to the kings of the whole world, to gather them for the battle on the great day of the God Almighty.'*

One may wonder if each one of those three evil spirits will play a part in the lives of those three kings, the King of the North, the King of the East and the King of the South. That could mean that those evil spirits would play a role in stirring those three kings to attack Israel given the present, ongoing tension in the Middle East?

This final battle described in Chapter 19, beginning with the heading: *The Rider on the White Horse* is described as follows:

11 I (John) saw heaven standing open and there before me was a white horse, whose rider is called Faithful and True. With justice He judges and makes war. 12 His eyes are like blazing fire, and on His head are many crowns. He has a name written on Him that no one knows but He Himself. 13 He is dressed in a robe dipped in blood, and His name is the Word of God. 14 The armies of heaven were following Him, riding on white horses and dressed in fine linen, white and clean. 15 Out of His mouth comes a sharp sword with which to strike down the nations. "He will rule them with an iron scepter." He treads the winepress of the fury of the wrath of God Almighty. 16 On His robe and on His thigh, He has this name written: KING OF KINGS AND LORD OF LORDS.

(Rev. 19:11-16).

17 And I saw an angel standing in the sun, who cried in a loud voice to all the birds flying in midair, "Come, gather together for the great supper of God, 18 so that you may eat the flesh of the kings, generals, and mighty men, of horses and their riders, and the flesh of all people, free and slave, small and great." 19 Then I saw the beast and the kings of the earth and their armies gathered together to make war against the rider on the horse and His army. 20 But the beast was captured, and with him the false prophet who had performed the miraculous signs on his behalf. With these signs he had deluded those who had received the mark of the beast and worshiped his image. The two of

them were thrown alive into the fiery lake of burning sulfur."
(Rev. 19:17-20).

It is remarkable that we read previously in the O.T. book Ezekiel
about that terrible and likely the final future battle at Armageddon. An
accompanying, even remarkable, observation that can be made is the
fact that Ezekiel describes a most important fact that speaks of the people of Israel following their official return to their God-given country in
1948 following 2000 years of exile.

Is Armageddon's Development foretold in the Bible, Ezekiel 18?
Read the following Bible verses:

14 "Therefore, son of man, prophesy and say to Gog: 'This is
what the Sovereign LORD says: In that day, when My people
Israel are living in safety, will you not take notice of it? 15 You
will come from your place in the far north (Russia?), you and
many nations with you, all of them riding on horses, a great
horde, a mighty army. 16 You will advance against My people
Israel like a cloud that covers the land. In days to come, O Gog,
I will bring you against My land, so that the nations may know
Me when I show Myself holy through you before their eyes...
(Ez. 38:14-16)

18 This is what will happen in that day: When Gog attacks
the land of Israel, My hot anger will be aroused, declares the
Sovereign LORD. 19 In My fiery wrath I will declare that at
the time there shall be a great earthquake in the land of Israel.
20 The fish of the sea, the birds of the air, the beasts of the field,
every creature that moves along the ground, and all the people
on the earth will tremble at My presence. The mountains will
be overturned, the cliffs will crumble, and every wall will fall to
the ground. (Ez. 38:18-20).

21 I will summon a sword against Gog on all My mountains, declares the Sovereign LORD. Every man's sword will be
against his brother. 22 I will execute judgment upon him with
plague and bloodshed; I will pour down torrents of rain, hail-

stones and burning sulfur on him and on his troops and on the many nations with him. 23 And so I will show My greatness and My holiness, and I will make Myself known in the sight of many nations. Then they will know that I am the LORD." (Ezek. 38: 21-23).

In her commentary on the OT book Zechariah[49], Joyce Baldwin explains,

> This book prepares God's people for the worst calamity they can ever face, the final triumph of evil over good. Even God's representative dies at the hand of evil men. There is no room in Zechariah's thinking for glib optimism, but when evil has done its worst the Lord remains King, and will be seen to be King by all the nations…what is urgent is that the whole book, after being fragmented for so long, should once again make its full impact on the church… Chapter 14 leaps to the day when the Lord will reign over all the earth, and so to the end of time (Zech. 14:7).[50]

But then, John Calvin wrote in his commentary on Zechariah, among other things, that Zechariah exhorted his people to persevere, while living in Babylonian Captivity/Exile (BCE 598--538 BCE).[51] Lately, we may listen to Zechariah, as he speaks of the coming of the LORD… a gathering of all the nations to Jerusalem to fight against it, capturing the city and doing great harm. Then the LORD will fight against those nations, His feet will stand on the Mount of Olives that will split in two from east to west. It will be a unique day, without daytime or nighttime, living water will flow out from Jerusalem.

Then we read also the following announcement,

---

[49] Joyce G. Baldwin, "*Haggai, Zechariah, Malachi*," Tyndale Old Testament Commentaries, Inter-Varsity Press, 1972.
[50] Joyce G. Baldwin, "*Haggai, Zechariah, Malachi*," Tyndale Old Testament Commentaries, Inter-Varsity Press, 1972, pp. 70, 71.
[51] John Calvin, "*Commentaries on the Twelve Minor Prophets, Vol. IV, HABAKKUK, ZEPHANIAH, HAGGAI*", Baker Book House, Grand Rapids, MI, Reprinted 1981.

The LORD will be king over the whole earth. On that day there will be one LORD, and His name the only name…Jerusalem will be raised up and remain in its place…it will be inhabited; never again will it be destroyed. Jerusalem will be secure. (Zech. 14:9-11).

The above words of Zech. 14:9-11 about the LORD and Jerusalem's future may bring us briefly back to the following words we read earlier on in Zechariah, Chapter 9,

9 "Rejoice greatly, O Daughter of Zion! Shout, Daughter of Jerusalem! See, your king comes to you, the righteous and having salvation, gentle and riding on a donkey. On a colt, the foul of a donkey…10b He will proclaim peace to the nations. His rule will extend from sea to sea and "from the river to the ends of the earth." (Zech. 9:9, 10b).

From reading these above words from Zechariah 9, we could draw the conclusion that he was pointing towards a period during which Jesus would spend time with His disciples, as we can read about in the four Gospels: Matthew, Mark, Luke and John. That means that Zechariah's vision may have spoken of Jesus' first coming (into) the world about 550 years into the future. However, Jesus, at that time, was not at all facing any significant, physical war, but more of a spiritual war leading eventually to His (physical) death on the cross.

A significant physical war came shortly after Jesus' death in 70 A.D. when Jerusalem and the Second Temple were destroyed by the Roman army, and Israelites were dispersed throughout the entire world. That could mean that the climactic battle of Armageddon was going to be during the so-called end times and before the time Jesus would return.

However, one or more questions can be raised about the so-called Battle of Armageddon. It is difficult to understand Jesus coming down from heaven to end that future war like a 'general leading his troops' to end the so-called future Armageddon war. According to Jesus' own words, He is supposed to come back to a completely and everlasting renewed earth, being not at all involved in any war. He Himself speaks of coming back to earth only once.

A conclusion from the above rhetoric about Jesus' appearance and final involvement in the ending of the War of Armageddon is that Jesus is not returning once, but twice. Before Jesus' self-proclaimed words of Him coming back after the destruction and following renewal of heavens and earth, after first His chosen ones (His Church) had joined Him, and together continue coming down from a renewed heaven to a renewed earth.

Then also, Jesus Himself has never mentioned the fact that He will first return to earth as a 'General ending the War of Armageddon', and a second time as the Lord of lords to gather all His chosen people in the air to begin everlasting life on a renewed earth.

Let me add another comment concerning a possible number of times Jesus is supposed to return. The following comment is based on Hanegraaff's novel, "Fuse of Armageddon." In this novel we hear of two persons, Quinn and Kate, who speak with each other, as the main players in the novel:

Quinn said to Kate,

The term dispensationalism is a method of biblical interpretation that says God's plan for mankind is divided into eras—dispensations—that will progress to the final end-times era. One of the foundations of this theology is that God will fulfill His promises to two peoples, namely believing Jews and believing Gentiles. p. 150.

This theology teaches that believers in Jesus will be 'raptured' to heaven during a secret coming of Christ, while nonbelievers will be left behind to face a seven-year global Tribulation, ending with another return of Christ to lead a victorious bloodbath against all His enemies at the Battle of Armageddon; then finally, after a thousand-year reign, Christ will in effect have another return to judge all the living and the dead of all mankind. pp.150-151.

Kate to Quinn,

Let me get this straight, a secret coming of Christ, and a third one at the end of a thousand years a return of Christ at Armageddon seven years later...it says in the New Testament that Jesus is coming back *three* different times? p. 152.[52]

In this novel, Hanegraaff makes the point that he disagrees with those who argue that Jesus seems to return more than once.

It is admitted that the above future developments are simple, direct interpretation of things expected to come. More discussions on that subject in Chapters Seven, Eight and Nine.

A Different Understanding of the Battle of Armageddon

Harry R. Boer explains that John envisioned Armageddon from a symbolic point of view.[53] Admitting that great battles have been fought on the Plain of Megiddo, he nevertheless understands the Battle of Armageddon, referred to in Rev. 16, 17 and 19, to be a symbol of the final meeting between the forces of good and of evil envisioned in Rev. 19,

> '*Then I saw the beast and the kings of the earth and their armies gathered together to make war against the rider on the horse and his army.*' (Rev.19:19).

When we, for example, turn to Rev. 19:11-16 we hear John saying that he saw,

> 11 *"heavens standing open and there before me was a white horse, whose rider is called Faithful and True. With justice He judges and makes war...* 13 *He is dressed in a robe dipped in blood, and His name is Word of God....*15 *Out of His mouth comes a sharp sword with which to strike down the nations...*16 *On His robe and on His thigh He has His name* written: *KING OF KINGS AND LORD OF LORDS.*' (Rev. 19:11, 13, 15-16).

[52] Hank Hanegraaff, *FUSE of Armageddon*, a novel, Tyndale, 2007.
[53] Harry R. Boer, *The Book Of Revelation*, William B. Eerdmans, Publishing Company Grand Rapids, Mi, 1979.

In this Bible passage reference is made to the Lord Jesus Christ, who had given His life on the cross, then 3 days later was resurrected from the death, and not long after had returned to His Father in heaven from where He reigns and eventually will judge the nations.

Harry Boer reminds us that Jesus had once said, *"All authority in heaven on earth has been given to Me"* (Matt. 28:19). It is this divine authority, not a new or an additional authority, He continues to govern the nations with a rod of iron…the basic character of this divine authority that enforces and maintains the law of God the Creator…Not much has been said about the battle of Armageddon itself concerning the time duration of that battle, and neither about the battle itself, including any planned assaults from the attacking forces. Then we are also left with the impression that this battle has not been a long one, as it seems to be a battle that will be suddenly and totally over and done with.

Boer also points out that the battle of Armageddon is placed at the end of the third and last cycle of judgments. When the last bowl has been poured out, a voice from the heavenly temple cries, 'It is done!' The seventh bowl brings us to the end of human history. Following a brief interlude, Boer then poses the question, "What does all this mean? In answering his own question he says the following,

> By Armageddon we understand a final confrontation between the forces of darkness and the forces of light, between those who are not of Christ and those who belong to Christ. While we have all kinds of physical aspects, the confrontation is basically spiritual in character.

Boer then also reminds us that we should not forget that with the story of Armageddon we are dealing with apocalyptic imagery, as he also reminds us, as I (Peter) understand, that this battle is to be a factor in the final test of strength between Christ and Satan, and thus between their respected followers.

Leaving many other observations concerning this end-time battle for any reader interested in Boer's insights, I repeat here the last question he raises at the very end of the Chapter on Armageddon,

How far off, how near, is the consummation that we have been contemplating? Who would dare say? But equally, who among those who discern the movements of history would dare to question that in our very time Armageddon is very much in the making?

However, we have already noticed earlier that peace talks are taking place, though also been interrupted, as of March, 2025. In the meantime, let me say this: It is only the last number of years that I began to put my head on the future with its final battle of Armageddon between two huge opposing armies in the Middle East. In my understanding, the location of such a battle would be a logical place, namely in the land of Israel. Israel, as a country, has been and still is God's personal choice for His original covenant people, the Israelites (Jews). Read Joshua 1:1-7.

This truth becomes more evident, since the Jewish people were officially allowed to return to their homeland in 1948, after they first were forced to leave their country and sent on their way all over the world in 70 AD. Since 1948, millions of Jews have returned to their God-given homeland. However, many of them have not yet turned in faith to God, and to His Son, Jesus Christ as their Lord and Savior. But at the same time, many of them, called Messianic Jews, have given their hearts to Jesus Christ. Hopefully, and very likely, many more will follow in the coming years.

Israel, as a country, has been, still is and remain God's personal choice for His original covenant people, the Israelites (Jews). Read Joshua 1:1-7.

We will again turn our attention to Hanegraaff's opinion concerning the Battle of Armageddon. This time, he approaches this Battle in the form of a figure of speech. He first refers to what the Bible says that,

at Armageddon the blood of Christ's enemies will rise "as high as the horses' bridles for a distance of 1,600 stadia." (Rev. 14:20).

Then, Hanegraaff continuous with the question if Scripture intends to convey, as LaHaye contends, that Palestine will be literally submerged in a five-food-deep river of blood that stretches the length of Palestine from north to south—or is the apostle John simply using an apocalyptic motif to convey massive wartime death and slaughter?[54]

I (Peter) would say that it is most likely the latter.

One may see the likelihood of a serious future battle, say the battle of Armageddon. That includes the notion that such a battle would take place in the land of Israel, as many previous battles have taken place in that very same area. One may certainly consider the possibility of a serious, future battle in that region, as we see the simmering hate from primarily Muslim countries around Israel, including the King of the North: Lebanon, Syria, or even Turkey, the King of the East: Iran, and the King of the South: Egypt with some other nearby Muslim countries, including South and West of Egypt, and/or Egypt itself. It could well be a final, decisive battle between Israel and most, if not all, surrounding Muslim nations.

In the meantime, we may wonder about the missing King of the West in that future battle. Is that because West of Israel we have the Mediterranean Sea? However, it could also mean, though less likely, that the Western world, including America and Europe, will not be involved in future's most important and final battle in the Middle East. That future battle seems to be contained to countries more closely around Israel.

At this moment in history, it is difficult to imagine that a present strong America, with Trump as President, though a friend of Israel, will be absent in such a future and final war, and so a rather weak Europe. That means that such a final war will not take place any time soon. Hmm.

We understand that in the future, these three Kings, very likely living in and/or near the Middle East, will signaling their hate for Israel. A future war between those three Kings and Israel is feasible, given past and present fights in the Middle East. We are now speaking about a possible future, physical battle between three Christ-denying countries against one country, Israel, that has presently many, if not most, Jews

---

[54] Hank Hanegraaff, "*FUSE of Armageddon*," a novel, Tyndale House Publishers, Inc, 2007.

who still have not accepted Christ as their Savior. But then, at the same time, many Jews have already embraced Jesus as their Lord and Savior. Even so, that important fact will have apparently no influence to hold off the reality of a coming devastating and final future war in the Middle East.

We also need to realize that those afore-mentioned Three Kings represent powerful, hateful anti-God, anti-Christ forces, as they could represent communism, radical Islamism, radical liberalism. These days, we have powerful Antichrist forces ready to turn so- called Christian countries, even continents, into bastions of anti-God countries. This is certainly the case in Western Europe, previously regarded as Christian nations.

Especially during the last thirty to forty years, the influence of China's communism, especially in higher education, has become apparent in many leadership positions within former Christian countries and continents. That points to the reality that Satan proves himself successful in influencing growing numbers of people in many of those original, well-functioning, Christian societies, including North America. That fact alone could explain why Western countries (i.e. no King of the West) will have, most likely, no input in the future, final battle in the Middle East.

Documentary: The Final War
At this point, I introduce the 21-minute documentary entitled: EXCLUSIVE DOCUMENTARY—The Final War Chapter 1: Post-Pandemic War.

Some introductory comments by Epoch Cinema, December 20, 2022,

> The Russia-Ukraine war; tension at the Taiwan Strait and the South China Sea; the Taliban's takeover of Afghanistan. Current world events may seem chaotic, but for the Chinese Communist Party (CCP), the central theme couldn't be clearer. These destabilizing factors provide the perfect opportunity for the CCP to reduce American power and build a new world order

that's friendlier to authoritarian regimes like itself. This chapter examines the CCP's role in recent global conflicts, as well as the regime's decades-long history of helping anti-American terrorists around the globe. We reveal the Communist Party's "evil tactics"—in the words of its own "state adviser"—to defeat America, as well as the "four enemies" the CCP tried to create to distract the United States.

Q. Why is the above-mentioned documentary important?

From the director of the viral documentary "Tracking Down the Origin of the Wuhan Coronavirus," "The Final War" is a documentary that uncovers the Chinese Communist Party's 100-year plot to defeat America. With exclusive research and personal stories from whistleblowers, the film reveals the CCP's plot behind the most-dire issues of our time: Taiwan, the Russia-Ukraine war, and the Taliban. Why is the CCP promoting the idea of "World War III"? What is the Party's long game against America? The answer is that "The Final War" answers the questions that are relevant to every American and Canadian (and maybe those living in Europe as well).

Spiritual and Physical Wars

Next to the above-mentioned documentary concerning a possible future physical war, we need to be aware of a present world-wide spiritual warfare that increasingly takes the form of pro-Christ versus anti-Christ forces. Having said this, we may go back to what Boer has said about Armageddon as a final confrontation between forces of darkness and those of light. That still leaves us with the question whether we will indeed experience a final physical or spiritual war in the (near) future.

At this point, I would like to suggest the possibility of a future Armageddon in the form of a spiritual battle between so called pro-Christ forces (Church) against anti-Christ (Satanic) forces. Such a possibility can be thought of, since so much of what we read in the Bible is about the contrast of God-obeying versus God-denying[55] forces.

---

[55] Gog, read e.g. Ezekiel 38, and Revelation 20 concerning Gog, chief prince of Meshech and Tubal.

One thing we can count on is that present spiritual battles throughout the world may grow more intense. Those battles will no longer involve certain parts of the world, but could, over time, involve a significant part of the world.

In the meantime, we can be sure that Satan continues to make life more difficult for Christians in the coming years. But then, the Lord Jesus Christ is with us, Christians, and so is the Holy Spirit, our present Counselor, both continuing to lead us how to get on with our lives, no matter what. But then again, how dedicated are todays and tomorrow's Christians, many of them young people? They need to learn and to be spiritually astute to face and endure ongoing, growing opposition from those who are enemies of Jesus Christ. In the meantime, we may wonder how many of us will realize such a possibility or fact.

CHAPTER SEVEN

THE RETURN (SECOND COMING) OF JESUS

"Blow the trumpet in Zion; sound the alarm on the holy hill. Let all who live in the land tremble" Joel 2:1a

THE GREAT COMMISSION

Jesus Farewell Words

According to Matthew 28,

> All authority in heaven and on earth has been given to me. Therefore, go and make disciples of all nations, baptizing them in the name of the Father and of the Son and of the Holt Spirit, and teaching them to obey everything I have commanded you. And surely, I am with you always, to the very end of the age. (Matt. 28:18-20).

According to Mark 16,

> Go into all the world and preach the good news to all creation. Whoever believes and is baptized will be saved, but whoever does not believe will be condemned. And these signs will accompany those who believe: In my name they will drive out demons; they will speak in new tongues; they will pick up snakes with their hands; and when they drink deadly poison, it will not hurt them at all; they will place their hands on sick people, and they will get well. (Mk. 16:15-18).

According to Luke 24,

> This is what is written: The Christ will suffer and rise from the dead on the third day, and repentance and forgiveness of sins will be preached in His name to all nations, beginning in Jerusalem. You are witnesses of these things. I am going to send you what My Father has promised; but stay in the city until you have been clothes with power from on high. (Lk. 24:46-49).

Jesus speaks of a Coming Destruction of Earth (Luke 21)

> 25 "There will be signs in the sun, moon and stars. On the earth, nations will be in anguish and perplexity at the roaring and tossing of the sea. 26 Men will faint from terror, apprehensive of what is coming on the world, for the heavenly bodies will be shaken. 27 At that time they will see the Son of man coming in a cloud with power and great glory. 28 When these things begin to take place, stand up and lift up your heads, because your redemption is drawing near." (Lk. 21:25-28).

The above 4 Bible passages seem to point to a future time prior to Jesus' return, after present heavens and earth will be destroyed and then renewed for everlasting time. Those Bible passages are not related to a possible future war of Armageddon, but to the time when Jesus returns to a completely renewed earth and heavens. At that time, Jesus will be accompanied by the many, (next page) already resurrected believers in Christ, meeting up with believers who are still alive at that time. (Rev. 21: 1-80).

In conjunction with the above Bible verses, we may listen to the following wonderful and encouraging words of Paul in his first letter to the Thessalonians, Chapter 4,

> 13 "Brothers, *we do not want you to be ignorant about those* who fall asleep, or to grieve like the rest of men, who have no hope. 14 We believe that Jesus died and rose again and so we believe

that God will bring with Jesus those who have fallen asleep in Him. 15 According to the Lord's own word, we tell you that we who are still alive, who are left till the coming of the Lord, will certainly not precede those who have fallen asleep. 16 For the Lord Himself will come down from heaven, with a loud command, with the voice of the archangel and with the trumpet call of God, and the dead in Christ will rise first. 17 After that, we who are still alive and are left will be caught up together with them in the clouds to meet the Lord in the air. And so, we will be with the Lord forever. 18 Therefore, encourage each other with these words." (1 Thess. 4:13-18).

THE RETURN of JESUS

Predictions concerning a first, secret, quiet Return of Jesus

The above Bible passage of 1 Thess. 4:13-18 is apparently used by La-Haye as a proof text in response to the widespread notion of a future "Rapture" of the church. That particular and sudden moment of a future "Rapture" is going to take place before the so called 'Tribulation' period of seven years.

As a matter of fact, there are currently two different theories about that Rapture theory. One theory tells us that there will be a future *pre*-Tribulation Rapture of the Church, another theory, according to Jeffrey, tells us that there will be a future *post*-Tribulation Rapture of the Church. In both rapture theories there will be a secret return of Christ, as well as a *seven-year Tribulation* period.

At one point in his study on the two theories, Hanegraaff reminds us of the fact that 'for nineteen hundred years, the idea of a pre-tribulation rapture was completely foreign to mainstream Christianity.'

Then, we also hear about the Plymouth Brethren who believe that the rapture and the return of Christ are going to be simultaneous events. Then Darby, according to historian Timothy Weber, developed the notion of a pre-tribulation rapture (of the Church). Darby apparently understood that the rapture and the second coming of Jesus are two separate events. At the rapture, Christ will come *for* his saints, and at His second coming He will come *with* his saints. Between these two events the great tribulation would occur.[56]

Hanegraaff's astute opinion about the pretext that there are two distinct phases in the second coming of Christ is little more than the product of fertile imagination…the faithful illumination of Scripture reveals neither a secret coming of Christ, followed by a seven-year Tribulation, nor a second chance for sin and salvation following the second coming of Christ. To the contrary, when Christ appears a second time, the kingdom that was inaugurated at the first appearing will be consummated in "a new heaven and a new earth, the home of righteousness." (2 Peter 3:13)[57]

More information on both rapture-theories can be found in Hanegraaff's book 'The Apocalypse Code, in which he also discusses topics such as: Two Distinct People, Two Distinct Plans, Two Distinct Phases.[58]

Biblical Predictions of events around Jesus' Future Return
The Day and Hour Unknown (Matthew 24)

> 36 "No one knows about that day or hour, not even the angels in heaven, nor the Son, but only the Father. 37 As it was in the days of Noah, so it will be at the coming of the Son of Man…39b That is how it will be at the coming of the Son of Man. 40 Two men will be in the field; one will be taken and the other left. 41 Two women will be grinding with a hand mill; one will be taken and the other left." (Matt. 24: 36-41). See also Luke 17:34-35.

Before the Sanhedrin (Matthew 26)

> 63b The high priest said to Him, "I charge You under oath by the living God: Tell us if You are the Christ, the Son of God."

---

[56] Hank Hanegraaff, *THE APOCALYPSE CODE*, Thomas Nelson, Nashville, Dallas,2007, 63.

[57] Ibid, 59-60.

[58] Hank Hanegraaff, *THE APOCALYPSE CODE*, Thomas Nelson, Nashville, Dallas, 2007, 48-69.

64 "Yes, it is as you say, "Jesus replied, "But I say to all of you: In the future you will see the Son of Man sitting at the right hand of the Mighty One and coming on the clouds of heaven." (Matt. 26:63b-64).

Signs of the End of the Age (Mark 13)

23 "So be on your guard; I have told you everything ahead of time. 24 "But in those days, following that distress, "'the sun will be darkened, and the moon will not give its light; 25 the stars will fall from the sky, and the heavenly bodies will be shaken.' 26 At that time men will see the Son of Man coming in clouds with great power and glory. 27 And He will send His angels and gather His elect from the four winds, from the ends of the earth to the ends of the heavens." (Mk. 13:23-27).

The Day and Hour Unknown (Mark 13)

32 "No one knows about that day or hour, not even the angels in heaven, nor the Son, but only the Father. 33 Be on guard! Be alert! You do not know when that time will come...36 If He comes suddenly, do not let Him find you sleeping. 37 What I say to you, I say to everyone: 'Watch!'"(Mk. 13:32-33; 36-37).

Jesus speaking to His Disciples (Luke 9).

26 If anyone is ashamed of Me and My words, the Son of Man will be ashamed of him when He comes in His glory and in the glory of the Father and of the holy angels. 27 I tell you the truth, some who are standing here will not taste death before they see the Kingdom of God. (Lk. 9:26-27).

The Coming of the Kingdom of God (Luke 17)
Jesus answer to the Pharisees' question when the kingdom would come, Jesus replied,

20b "The kingdom of God does not come with your careful observation, 21 nor will people say, 'Here it is,' or 'There it is,'" because the kingdom of God is within you." (Lk. 17:20-21).

Following His above-mentioned reply to that Pharisees' question, Jesus continued to explain in the next 14 verses, Luke 17:22-36, how suddenly, and un-expectantly, His return would be (see next pages 217-219).

Watchfulness (Luke 12)

40 You also must be ready, because the Son of Man will come at an hour when you do not expect Him." (Lk. 12:40).

Jesus is Coming Back (Revelation 21)

12 Behold, I am coming soon! My reward is with Me, and I will give to everyone according to what he has done, 13 I am the Alpha and the Omega, the First and the Last, the Beginning and the End. 14 Blessed are those who wash their robes, that they may have the right to the tree of life and may go through the gates into the city. 15 Outside are the dogs, those who practice magic arts, the sexually immoral, the murderers, the idolaters and everyone who loves and practices falsehood...20 "He who testifies to these things says, "Yes, I am coming soon. (Rev. 21:12-15, 20).

The Return of the Lord (2 Thessalonians)

1 Now, brothers, about times and dates we do not need to write to you, 2 for you know well that the day of the Lord will come like a thief in the night. 3 While people are saying, "Peace and safety," destruction will come on them suddenly, as labor pains on a pregnant woman, and they will not escape...6 So then, let us not be like others, who are asleep, but let us be alert and

self-controlled...8 ...putting on faith and love as a breastplate, and the hope of salvation as a helmet. (2 Thess. 5: 1-8).

The Resurrection of the Dead (1 Corinthians 15)

1 For since death came through one man, the resurrection of the dead also through a man. 22 For as in Adam all die, so in Christ all will be made alive. 23 But each in his own turn: Christ: the first fruits; then, when He comes, those who belong to Him. 24 Then the end will come, when He hands over the kingdom to God the father after He has destroyed all dominion, authority and power. 25 For he must reign until He has put all His enemies under His feet. 26 For the last enemy to be destroyed is death. (1 Cor. 15: 21-26).

The Resurrection of the Body (1 Corinthians 15)

42 So will it be with the resurrection of the dead. The body that is sown is perishable, it is raised imperishable; 43 it is sown in weakness, it is raised in power; 44 it is sown a natural body, it is raised a spiritual body. (1 Cor. 15: 42-44).

50 "I declare to you brothers, that flesh and blood cannot inherit the kingdom of God, nor does the perishable inherit the imperishable. 51 Listen, I tell you a mystery: We will not all sleep, but we will all be changed—in a flash, in the twinkling of an eye, at the last trumpet. For the trumpet will sound, the dead will be raised imperishable, and we will be changed." (1 Cor. 15: 50-52).

Our Heavenly Dwelling (2 Corinthians 5)

1 Now we know that if the earthly tent we live in is destroyed, we have a building from God, an eternal house in heaven, not built by human hands... 5 Now it is God who has made us for this very purpose and had given us the Spirit as a deposit,

guaranteeing what is to come… 10 For we must appear before the judgement seat of Christ, that each one may receive what is due him for the things done while in the body, whether good or bad. (2 Cor. 5: 1, 5, 10).

Make Alive in Christ (Ephesians 2)

6 And God raised us up with Christ and seated us with Him in the heavenly realms in Christ Jesus, 7 in order that in the coming ages He might show the incomparable riches of His grace, expressed in His kindness to us in Christ Jesus. (Eph. 2:6-7).

Pressing on Toward the Goal (Philippians 3)

20 But our citizenship is in heaven. And we eagerly await a Savior from there, the Lord Jesus Christ, 21 who, by the power that enables Him to bring everything under His control, will transform our lowly bodies so that they will be like His glorious body." (Phil. 3: 21-22).

THE COMING ETERNAL REIGN OF JESUS

Old Testament and New Testament Predictions
One Old-Testament foretelling (Zechariah 8)
In O.T. book of Zechariah 8 we read,

This is what the LORD says: I will return to Zion and dwell in Jerusalem. Then Jerusalem will be called the City of Truth, and the mountain of the LORD Almighty will be called the Holy Mountain. (Zech. 8:3).

Signs of the End of the Age (Matthew 24)

3 As Jesus was sitting on the Mount of Olives, the disciples came to Him privately. "Tell us, they said, "when will this hap-

pen, and what will be the sign of your coming and the end of the age?

4 Jesus responding to His disciples, Watch out that no one deceives you. 5 For many will come in my name, claiming, 'I am the Christ, and will deceive many. 6 You will hear of wars and rumors of wars but see to it that you are not alarmed. Such things must happen, but the end is still to come. 7 Nations will rise against nations, and kingdom against kingdom. There will be famines and earthquakes in various places. 8 All these are the beginning of birth pains. (Matt. 24:4-8).

29 Immediately after the distress of those days "'the sun will be darkened, and the moon will not give its light; the stars will fall from the sky, and the heavenly bodies will be shaken.' 30 "At that time the sign of the Son of Man will appear in the sky, and all the nations of the earth will mourn. They will see the Son of man coming on the clouds of the sky, with power and great glory. 31 And He will send His angels with a loud trumpet call, and they will gather His elect from the four winds, from one end of the heaven to the other. (Matt. 24:29-31).

Note: Mark 13:24-27 matches Matt. 24: 29-31.
Jesus speaking (Revelation 22)

12 Behold, I am coming soon! My reward is with Me, and I will give to everyone according to what he has done. 13 I am the Alpha and the Omega, the First and the Last, the Beginning and the End. 14 Blessed are those who wash their robes, that they may have the right to the tree of life and may go through the gates into the city. 15 Outside are the dogs, those who practice magic arts, the sexual immoral, the murderers, the idolaters and everyone who loves and practices falsehood. (Rev. 22:12-15).

Prior to the Day of the Lord (the Lord's Second Coming)
• Church: walk in purity.

- Spirit of Scoffing: culture growing cold toward values, the truth, God.
- The Day of the Lord: 2 Peter 3:1-10; 2 Peter 3: 11-18.

See also Rev. 21:1-3; Joel 2:28-32.

The Call to Persevere (Hebrews 10) 22 Let us draw near to God with a sincere heart in full assurance of faith, having our hearts sprinkled to cleanse us from a guilty conscience and having our bodies washed with pure water. 23 Let us hold unswervingly to the hope we profess, for He who promised is faithful. 24 And let us consider how we may spur one another on toward love and good deeds. 25 Let us not give up on meeting together, as some are in the habit of doing, but let us encourage one another—and even more as you see the day approaching. (Hebr. 10:22-25).

Final Warning (Revelation 22)
The apostle John speaking again,

> And if anyone takes words away from this book of prophecy, God will take away from him his share in the tree of life and in the holy city, which are described in this book. (Rev. 22:19).

The Armor of God (Ephesians 6)

> 10 Finally, be strong in the lord and in His mighty power. 11 Put on the full armor of God so that you can take your stand against the devil's schemes. 12 For our struggle is not against flesh and blood, but against the authorities, against the rulers, against the authorities, against the powers of this dark world and against the spiritual forces of evil in the heavenly realms. 13 Therefore put on the full armor of God. So that when the day of evil comes, you may be able to stand your ground, and after you have done everything, to stand. 14 Stand firm then, with the belt of truth...the breastplate of righteousness...15 with your feet fitted with the readiness that comes from the gospel of peace...16 take up the shield of faith...17 take the helmet of

salvation and sword of the Spirit which is the word of God. 18 And pray in the Spirit on all occasions with all kinds of prayers and requests. Be alert and always keep on praying for all the saints. (Eph. 6: 10-18).

The New Jerusalem (Revelation 21)
The apostle John speaking,

1 Then I saw a new heaven and a new earth, for the first heaven and the first earth had passed away, and there was no longer any sea (i.e. no more unrest, 2 I saw the Holy City, the New Jerusalem (i.e. the Church, including all Messianic Jews and Gentiles, addition mine), coming down out of heaven from God, prepared as a bride beautifully dressed for her husband. 3 And I heard a loud voice from the throne saying,

"Now the dwelling of God is with men, and He will live with them. They will be His people, and God Himself will be with them and be their God. 4 He will wipe every tear from their eyes. There will be no more death or mourning or crying or pain, for the old order of things has passed away. (Rev. 21:1-4).

Thanksgiving and Prayer (2 Thessalonians 1)

...among God's churches we boast about your perseverance and faith in all the persecutions and trials you are enduring. 5 All this is evidence that God's judgement is right, and as a result you will be counted worthy of the kingdom of God, for which you are suffering. 6 God is just: He will pay back trouble to those who trouble you 7 and give relief to you who are troubled, and to us as well. This will happen when the Lord Jesus is revealed from heaven in blazing fire with powerful angels. (Thess. 1: 4-7).

The above overview of many Bible passages, taken from mostly the New Testament, is a wonderful testimony regarding the coming, future reality of our Lord Jesus Christ's return to a completely restored, earth to start the promised eternal life of Christ and His Church, His Bride. What an enormous joy that moment, that everlasting life, will give us and always will be with us.

Chapter 21, 22 I did not see a temple in the city, because the Lord God Almighty and the Lamb are its temple. 23 The city does not need the sun or the moon to shine on it, for the glory of God gives it light, and the Lamb is its light, and the kings of the earth will bring their splendor into it. 24 The nations will walk by its light, and the kings of the earth will bring their splendor into it. 25 On no day will its gates ever be shut, for there will be no night there. 26 The glory and honor of the nations will be brought into it. 27 Nothing impure will ever enter it, nor will anyone who does what is shameful or deceitful, but only those whose names are written in the Lamb's book of life. (Rev. 21:22-27).

The Third Temple and the Antichrist

Many Christians and Jews are anxiously awaiting the building of a Third Temple in Jerusalem (see also p. 59), and about a coming, lasting building, one of a spiritual nature, that points to Christ's Church. In his letter to the Ephesians, Paul wrote,

> 19...you are no longer foreigners and aliens, but fellow citizens with God's people and members of God's household, 20 built on the foundation of the apostles and prophets, with Christ Jesus Himself as the chief cornerstone. 21 In Him the whole building is joined together and rises to become a holy temple in the Lord. 22 And in Him you too are being built together to become a dwelling in which God lives by His Spirit. (Ephesians 2: 19-2)2.

Revelation 22 says,

> 3 No longer will there be any curse. The throne of God and of the Lamb will be in the city, and His servants will serve Him. 4 They will see His face, and His name will be on their foreheads. 5 There will be no more night. They will not need the light of

a lamp or the light of the sun, for the Lord God will give them light. And they will reign for ever and ever." (Rev. 22:3-5).

My personal understanding is that the so-called Third Temple is not to be understood as a man-made building, but to be God's chosen people, i.e. all true believers in Christ. That fact leads us to ask how we need to understand that this Antichrist person will enter the Third Temple, as the latter is understood as referring to all followers of Jesus Christ. This then leads us to wonder how we need to understand that, and how, the Antichrist will enter the one worldwide body believers in Christ to lead them astray from Christ?

Considering the above-mentioned question, we may wonder whether this so-called Antichrist is indeed a real person. Could it be that this Antichrist could be a most dangerous, Christ-opposing spirit, who will create significant havoc throughout the world and especially among the world-wide body of believers?

Considering this last question, we may listen to what we read in the Bible concerning the Antichrist, also referred to as the Man of Lawlessness,

Concerning the coming of our Lord Jesus Christ and our being gathered to Him, we ask you, brothers, 2 not to become easily unsettled or alarmed by some prophecy, report or letter supposed to have come from us…3 Don't let anyone deceive you in any way, for that day will not come until the rebellion occurs and the man of lawlessness is revealed, the man doomed to destruction. 4 He will oppose and will exalt himself over everything that is called God or is worshiped, so that he sets himself up in God's temple, proclaiming himself to be God. (2 Thess. 2:1-4).

Revelation 13:18

This calls for wisdom. If anyone has insight, let him calculate the number of the beast, for it is man's number. His number is 666.

Conclusion: The number **666** means that: **This Beast is Satan.**

CHAPTER EIGHT

NEW HEAVEN(S) AND A NEW EARTH

OLD TESTAMENT on the New Heavens and a New Earth.

New Heavens and a New Earth (Isaiah 65)

Behold, I will create new heavens and a new earth. The former things will not be remembered, nor will they come to mind. 18 But be glad and rejoice forever in what I will create, for I will create Jerusalem to be a delight and its people a joy. 19 I will rejoice over Jerusalem and take delight in my people; the sound of weeping and of crying will be heard in it no more. 20 Never again will there be in it an infant who lives but a few days, or an old man who does not live out his years; he who dies at a hundred will be thought a mere youth; he who fails to reach a hundred will be considered accursed. (Isaiah 65: 17-20).

21 They will build houses and dwell in them; they will plant vineyards and eat their fruit. 22 No longer will they build houses and others live in them, or plant and others eat. For as the days of a tree, so will be the days of My people; My chosen ones will long enjoy the work of their hands. 23 They will not toil in vain, or bear children doomed to misfortune; for they will be a people blessed by the LORD, they and their descendants with them. 24 Before they call, I will answer; while they are still speaking, I will hear. 25 The wolf and the lamb will feed together, and the lion will eat straw like the ox, but dust will be the serpent's food. They will neither harm nor destroy on all my holy mountain. Says the LORD. (Isa. 65:21-25).

To understand this OT description of the 'New Heavens and a New Earth,' (see p.217) four OT commentaries on this Bible passage of Isa. 65:17-25 have been checked. May the following brief comments, made by the next four people, be helpful in reaching a good, satisfying understanding of the New Heavens and Earth.

John Calvin: This passage is about restoring His Church in such a manner that it shall appear as to gain new life. Isaiah speaks of the restoration of the Church after the return from Babylon towards the restoration of former times, thus causing great joy and no longer will remember their past miseries. God will partake in their joy, whether they are children or old men…. always being vigorous like people in their prime of life.[59]

J. A. Alexander: Isaiah speaks of an entire change in the existing state of things…implying the oblivion of the former state of things being much more naturally, connected with moral and spiritual changes than with one of a material nature. These Bible verses give us a poetical description of a complete and glorious change…poetical description of longevity, to be explained precisely like the promise of new heavens and a new earth…predictions to be figuratively understood.[60]

Edward J. Young: This Bible passage is about creating something fundamentally new, a new work of creation in which heavens and earth are employed as figures to indicate a complete renovation or revelation in the existing course of affairs. Paul shows how the new creation applies to believers: 2 Cor. 5:17; Gal. 6:15, see also Hebr. 2:5 and 2 Pet. 3:15. One of the blessings of the new age is that of longevity. Blessing of the new age characterizes the Messianic Age.[61]

R. N. Whybray: This Bible passage shows an entire lack of a detailed description characteristic of the apocalyptic predictions of the end of the new creation. It marks the beginning of a new radical theology, born of the despair of post-exilic life. When Yaweh creates, it

---

[59] John Calvin, "*Calvin's Commentaries*," Volume VIII, Baker Book House, Grand Rapids, Michigan, 1981.

[60] J. A. Alexander, "*The Prophecies of Israel*," Zondervan Publishing House, Grand Rapids, MI, 1978.

[61] Edward J. Young, "*The Book of Isaiah*," Volume III, William B. Eerdmans Publishing Company, Grand Rapids, 1981.

is always something quite new. For the Israelites: long life was one of the signs of God's blessing, and early death often attributed to sin. Regarding, 'A child shall die a hundred years old,' signifies a promise of a return to the legendary longevity of the age before the Flood recorded in Genesis. Longevity: healthy and useful life.

Upon reading these four short comments on Isa. 65:17-25, we may come at least to the conclusion that this OT passage in Isiah 65 is not at all referring to the NT passage of Rev. 21:1-7 that follows below. This understanding prevents any confusion between the two Bible passages on the 'New Heavens and New Earth' found in both Testaments. To me, John Calvin's understanding of this Bible passage to be the proper one.

NEW TESTAMENT on the New Heavens and a New Earth

> For the lord Himself will come down from heaven, with a loud command, with the voice of the archangel and with the trumpet call of God, and the dead in Christ will rise first. After that, we who are still alive and are left will be caught up together with them in the clouds to meet the Lord in the air. And so we will be with the Lord forever. (1 Thess. 4:16).

2 Peter 3 (The Day of the Lord)

> 3 First of all, you must understand that in the last days scoffers will come, scoffing and following their own evil desires. 4 They will say, "Where is this 'coming' He promised? Ever since our fathers died, everything goes on as it has since the beginning of creation." 5 But they deliberately forget that long ago by God's word the heavens existed, and the earth was formed out of water and by water. 6 By these waters also the world of that time was deluged and destroyed. 7 By the same word the present heavens and earth are reserved for fire, being kept for the Day of Judgment and the destruction of ungodly men. (2 Peter3: 3-7).

10 But the day of the Lord will come like a thief. The heavens will disappear with a roar; the elements will be destroyed by fire, and the earth and everything in it will be laid bare. 11 Since everything will be destroyed in this way, what kind of people ought you to be? You ought to live holy and godly lives 12 as you look forward to the day of God and speed its coming. That day will bring about the destruction of the heavens by fire, and the elements will melt in the heat. 13 But in keeping with His promise we are looking forward to a new heaven and a new earth, the home of righteousness. (2 Pet. 10:3-1).

Revelation 21 (The New Jerusalem)

1 Then I (John) saw a new heaven and a new earth, for the first heaven and the first earth had passed away, and there was no longer any sea (i.e. unrest). 2 I saw the Holy City, the New Jerusalem, coming down out of heaven from God, prepared as a bride beautifully dressed for her husband. 3 And I heard a loud voice from the throne saying, "Now the dwelling of God is with men, and He will live with them. They will be His people, and God Himself will be with them and be their God. 4 He will wipe every tear from their eyes. There will be no more death or mourning or crying or pain, for the old order of things has passed away." 5 He who was seated on the throne said, "I am making everything new! Then He said, "write this down, for these words are trustworthy and true." 6 He said to me: "It is done. I am the Alpha and the Omega, the Beginning and the End. To him who is thirsty I will give to drink without costs from the spring of the water of life. 7 He who overcomes will inherit all this, and he will be his God, and he will be My song. (Rev. 21:1-7.

Several Observation

The difference in the descriptions of the new heaven(s) and earth in the OT and NT raises the interesting question about the seemingly different period the OT and NT speak of. While the former (OT) speaks of people living long lives, but still will die, the latter (NT) speaks of lasting life, and thus no death anymore. That difference tells us that the Old Testament could speak of new heavens and a new earth thereby pointing to a different period than the time period we hear about in the New Testament.

As there are many voices in various circles speak of the New Jerusalem as a real, renewed, large and everlasting city, we may read Rev. 21: 2, to understand that the New Jerusalem will not be a city of stone, but the one, everlasting Church, the Bride of Christ.

The following observations can be made: The prophet Isaiah wrote his prophetic letter during the period 701 B.C. and 681 B.C, while Paul, Peter and John's letters were written before AD 70, except for Revelation. That means that there is a significant period between the OT and NT prophetic descriptions of a future new havens and earth. Both prophetic descriptions were written during difficult times: the former related to Assyrian oppression, the latter related to the imminent Roman oppression. Nevertheless, both OT and NT messages were inspired by the triune God.

Growing Threat of Global Destruction

There is a growing stockpile of nuclear warheads around the world. One graphic shows Russia having 15,000 warheads, the United States: 10,000; France: 450; China: 200-400; United Kingdom: 200; Israel: 75-200; India: 50; Pakistan: 50; North Korea: unknown.[62]

Note: These numbers will be so much higher today given the fact that those estimates were made in 2018, i.e. 7 years earlier.

The above figures of a great arsenal of destructive weapons seem to tell us that our present world could be destroyed at any time. This reality makes us also realize that God's Word about the destruction of this world is certainly not an innocent threat that can be easily dismissed as a kind of serious warning. In both the OT and the NT, we read about a serious divine warning that not only the world, but also the entire universe (cosmos) will be temporarily destroyed. Listen to the following biblical warnings in Isaiah 34. (see next page 233).

---

[62] Richard F. Ames, *ARMAGEDDON and BEYOND*, Living Church of Christ, 2018

Isaiah 34,

1 Come near, you nations, and listen; pay attention, you peoples! Let the earth hear, and all that is in it, the world, and all that comes out of it! 2 The LORD is angry with all nations; His wrath is upon all their armies. He will totally destroy them; He will give them over to slaughter. 3 Their slain will be thrown out; their dead bodies will send up a stench; the mountains will be soaked with their blood. 4 All the stars of the heavens will be dissolved and the sky rolled up like a scroll; all the starry host will fall like withered leaves from the vine, like shriveled figs from the fig tree." (Isa. 34:1-4).

Peter 3,

10 But the day of the Lord will come like a thief. The heavens will disappear with a roar; the elements will be destroyed by fire, and the earth and everything in it will be laid bare. 11 Since everything will be destroyed in this way, what kind of people ought you to be? You ought to live holy and godly lives 12 as you look forward to the day of God and speed its coming. That day will bring about the destruction of the heavens by fire, and the elements will melt in the heat. 13 But in keeping with His promise we are looking forward to a new heaven and a new earth, the home of righteousness. (2 Pet. 3:10-13).

We may wonder when that future destruction of our present, troubled world, including the surrounding universe, will happen. There certainly will be an enormous spectacle before God brings in a completely new world, and thereby a completely renewed universe as well. From Peter's Second letter we learn that the coming, monumental and mind-boggling destruction will involve present heavens and earth. This coming destruction is difficult to comprehend, and to form helpful ideas about the new reality of the future renewed earth and heaven(s).

Scriptures about the End of this Age

Let's also take note of what we read about the End of this Age in the Gospels of Matthew and Luke.

In Matthew 24 we read,

> 21 "For then there will be great distress, unequaled from the beginning of the world until now—and never to be equaled again. 22 If those days had not been cut short, no one would survive, but for the sake of the elect those days will be shortened....27 "For as lightning that comes from the east is visible even in the west, so will be the coming of the Son of Man...29 Immediately after the distress of those days 'the sun will be darkened, and the moon will not give its light; the stars will fall from the sky, and the heavenly bodies will be shaken.'
>
> 30 At that time the sign of the Son of Man will appear in the sky, and all the nations of the earth will mourn. They will see the Son of Man coming on the clouds of the sky, with power and great glory. 31 And He will send His angels with a loud trumpet call, and they will gather His elect from the four winds, from one end of the heavens to the other...44 So you also must be ready, because the Son of Man will come at an hour when you do not expect Him. (Matt. 24: 21-22; 27; 29-31; 44).

In Luke 21 we read,

> 25 There will be signs in the sun, moon and stars. On the earth, nations will be in anguish and perplexity at the roaring and tossing of the sea. 26 Men will faint from terror, apprehensive of what is coming on the world, for the heavenly bodies will be shaken. 27 At that time they will see the Son of man coming in a cloud with power and great glory. (Lk. 21:25-27).

Jesus' Return following the Global-wide Destruction

It is understood that such an enormous scale of destruction, as described in forenamed Bible passages, will take place around Jesus' Second Coming. Jesus' future return will include the presence of all His elect (Messianic Jews and Gentiles together, forming the True Church, i.e. all Messianic believers, obedient followers of Christ in all matters of life.

The Bible also explains that Jesus' elected ones, having died before His Final Coming, will meet Jesus during His return to earth, while enjoying their renewed, eternal bodies. As such, they will accompany Jesus when He continues to come down towards a renewed earth. During that descent, they will meet the elected ones who were still alive during the time of Jesus' return to earth. By the time of that meeting, those believers will then also have received their renewed, everlasting bodies. Then Jesus, together with His united Church, will (eventually) continue to descend to a completely renewed earth on which they will begin their everlasting lives.

One remaining question that we may arise considering Jesus' return, accompanied by His ransomed Church is this: when, or at what period will the coming catastrophic destruction and renewal of heavens and earth take place? It seems that all Jesus-elected men, women, and children, still living on earth prior to Jesus' return, will most likely be away from the earth to meet their descending Lord Jesus Christ (the 'rapture') and those Christians who are already with Jesus. Jesus, together with His One everlasting Church, the New Jerusalem, His future Bride.

Before that final return to earth, Jesus and His Church (all true followers of Jesus in their lasting transformed bodies) being together in midair between heavens and earth, will stay safely away from the ongoing, enormous calamity of heavens and earth. When that enormous calamity is over, Jesus and His Church will make their descend to the renewed earth where they will enjoy their eternal lives together.

How to read e.g. 2 Peter 3:10-13 quoted above. How do we need to understand Matt. 24:30, 31 in that light?

The End of Satan and Demons

In Revelation 20 we hear about Satan's doom as follows,

> 7 When the thousand years are over, Satan will be released from his prison 8 and will go out to deceive the nations in the

four corners of the earth—Gog and Magog—to gather them for battle. In number they are like the sand on the seashore. 9 They marched across the breath of the earth and surrounded the camp of God's people, the city he loves. But fire came down from heaven and devoured them. 10 And the devil, who deceived them, was thrown into the lake of burning sulfur, where the beast and the false prophet had been thrown. They will be tormented day and night for ever and ever. (Rev. 20:7-10).

CHAPTER NINE
RETROSPECT

Introduction

Chapters Four to Seven of the book of Revelation are about events during the post-Christian Era. Finally, Chapter Eight speaks of the New Heavens and the New Earth that will be enjoyed by those who belong to Jesus Christ, as we hear in Revelation, Chapter 21,

> 1 Then I (John) saw a new heaven and a new earth, for the first earth had passed away, and there was no longer any sea (i.e. unrest). 2 I saw the Holy City, the New Jerusalem, coming down out of heaven from God, prepared as a bride beautifully dressed for her husband. 3 And I heard a loud voice from the throne saying, "Now the dwelling of God is with men, and He will live with them. They will be His people, and God Himself will be with them and be their God. 4 He will wipe every tear from their eyes. There will be no more death or mourning or crying or pain, for the old order of things has passed away. (Rev. 21:1-4).

From this Bible passage we understand that the coming New Jerusalem is not to be a renewed city of Jerusalem the way we know about the present city of Jerusalem, but is a description of all, unwavering, believers in Jesus Christ, prepared as the Bride of Jesus.

THREE DIFFERENT TIME PERIODS

Earlier, in Chapter Four, Jonathan Cahn explains that there are three different, subsequent, time periods in world history, including pre-Christian,

Christian and post-Christian civilizations. Cahn then explained the differences between pre-Christian, Christian, and post-Christian eras. Based on those different time periods in world history we may thereby also think about three different, subsequent time episodes in creation. Let me explain as follows:

Past: First Time Period (Episode): <u>Sinless Creation</u>: Heavens, earth, man and angels.

In Genesis 1, we hear about the initial creation of the heavens and earth by the triune God (note the plural "let us"). Then, in verse 26, God said,

> Let us make man in our image, in the image of God He created Him; male and female He created them…

Then we read in Genesis 2,

> Thus, the heavens and earth were completed in all their vast array. Gen. 2:1.

In this first episode of creation, we also read in Gen. 2:4-25 about the creation of the first two persons, Adam and Eve, man and woman, both without sin, initially.

Present: Second Time Period (Episode): <u>Sinful Creation</u>: Mankind and angels (both good and bad angels (demons).

Genesis 3 explains how mankind fell into sin, remained and kept their sinful nature throughout the entire Bible period unto Revelation 21, that speaks of the New Jerusalem. During that earthly period Jesus is building His one and only Church consisting of so called Messianic (Jews and Gentiles), all true believers in Christ.

Future: Third Time Period (Episode): Completely Renewed & <u>Everlasting Creation</u>:

In 1 Thessalonians 4 we read,

> 16 For the lord Himself will come down from heaven, with a loud command, with the voice of the archangel and with the

trumpet call of God, and the dead in Christ will rise first. 17 After that, we who are still alive will be caught up together with them in the clouds to meet the Lord in the air. And so we will be with the erefore encourage each other with these words. (Thess. 4:16-18).

Rejoice in the Lord always. I will say it again: Rejoice! 5 Let your gentleness be evident to all. The Lord is nearby. 6 Do not be anxious about anything, but in everything, by prayer and petition, with thanksgiving, present your requests to God. 7 And the peace of God, which transcends all understanding, will guard your hearts and your minds in Christ Jesus. 8 Finally, brothers, whatever is true, whatever is noble, whatever is right, whatever is pure, whatever is lovely, whatever is admirable—if anything is excellent or praiseworthy—think about such things. 9 Whatever you have learned or received or heard from me or in me—put it into practice. And the God of peace will be with you." (Phil. 4:4-9).

APPPENDIX A
BIBLE VERSES CONCERNING SEXUAL MMORALITY

Note: Following Scripture quotations are mainly taken from The Holy Bible, English Standard Version (ESV). Copyright ©2001 by Crossway Bibles. Quotations from Jesus' words are taken from the NIV.

OLD TESTAMENT
Genesis 1:28,

> And God blessed them. And God said to them, "Be fruitful and multiply and fill the earth and subdue it and have dominion over the fish of the sea and over the birds of the heavens and over every living thing that moves on the earth.

Genesis 2:24,

> "*Therefore, a man shall leave his father and his mother and hold fast to his wife, and they shall become one flesh.*"

Exodus 20:14,

> "*You shall not commit adultery.*"

Leviticus 18:1-5,

> And the Lord spoke to Moses, saying, "Speak to the people of Israel and say to them, I am the Lord your God. You shall

not do as they do in the land of Egypt, where you lived, and you shall not do as they do in the land of Canaan, to which I am bringing you. You shall not walk in their statutes. You shall follow my rules and keep my statutes and walk in them. I am the Lord your God. You shall therefore keep my statutes and my rules; if a person does them, he shall live by them: I am the Lord.

Leviticus 18:22-23,

You shall not lie with a male as with a woman; it is an abomination. And you shall not lie with any animal and so make yourself unclean with it, neither shall any woman give herself to an animal to lie with it: it is perversion.

Leviticus 20:10,

If a man commits adultery with the wife of his neighbor, both the adulterer and the adulteress shall surely be put to death.

Leviticus 20:13,

If a man lies with a male as with a woman, both have committed an abomination; they shall surely be put to death; their blood is upon them.

Leviticus 20:15-16,

If a man lies with an animal, he shall surely be put to death, and you shall kill the animal. If a woman approaches any animal and lies with it, you shall kill the woman and the animal; they shall surely be put to death; their blood is upon them.

Deuteronomy 22:30,

A man shall not take his father's wife, so that he does not uncover his father's nakedness.

Deuteronomy 23:17-18,

None of the daughters of Israel shall be a cult prostitute, and none of the sons of Israel shall be a cult prostitute. You shall not bring the fee of a prostitute or the wages of a dog into the house of the Lord your God in payment for any vow, for both are an abomination to the Lord your God.

Proverbs 2:16-19,

So you will be delivered from the forbidden woman, from the adulteress with her smooth words, who forsakes the companion of her youth and forgets the covenant of her God; for her house sinks down to death, and her paths to the departed; none who go to her come back, nor do they regain the paths of life.

Proverbs 5:1-5,

My son, be attentive to my wisdom; incline your ear to my understanding, that you may keep discretion, and your lips may guard knowledge. For the lips of a forbidden woman drip honey, and her speech is smoother than oil, but in the end, she is bitter as wormwood, sharp as a two-edged sword. Her feet go down to death; her steps follow the path to Sheol.

Proverbs 5:18-19,

Let your fountain be blessed, and rejoice in the wife of your youth, a lovely deer, a graceful doe. Let her breasts fill you at all times with delight; be intoxicated always in her love.

Proverbs 6:26-29,

For the price of a prostitute is only a loaf of bread, but a married woman hunts down a precious life. Can a man carry fire next to his chest and his clothes not be burned? Or can one walk on hot coals and his feet not be scorched? So is he who goes in to his neighbor's wife; none who touches her will go unpunished.

Proverbs 6:32,

He who commits adultery lacks sense; he who does it destroys himself.

Proverbs 7:1-5,

My son, keep my words and treasure up my commandments with you; keep my commandments and live; keep my teaching as the apple of your eye; bind them on your fingers; write them on the tablet of your heart. Say to wisdom, "You are my sister," and call insight your intimate friend, to keep you from the forbidden woman, from the adulteress with her smooth words.

Jeremiah 23:14,

But in the prophets of Jerusalem, I have seen a horrible thing: they commit adultery and walk in lies; they strengthen the hands of evildoers, so that no one turns from his evil; all of them have become like Sodom to me, and its inhabitants like Gomorrah.

NEW TESTAMENT
Matthew 5:32,

You have heard that it was said, 'You shall not commit adultery.' But I say to you that everyone who looks at a woman with lustful intent has already committed adultery with her in his heart.

But I say to you that everyone who divorces his wife, except on the ground of sexual immorality, makes her commit adultery, and whoever marries a divorced woman commits adultery.

Matthew 19:1-5,

Now when Jesus had finished these sayings, he went away from Galilee and entered the region of Judea beyond the Jordan. And large crowds followed him, and he healed them there. And Pharisees came up to him and tested him by asking, "Is it lawful to divorce one's wife for any cause? He answered, have you not read that he who created them from the beginning made them male and female, and said,

Therefore, a man shall leave his father and his mother and hold fast to his wife, and the two shall become one flesh?

Matthew 19:9,

And I say to you: whoever divorces his wife, except for sexual immorality, and marries another, commits adultery.

Mark 7:20-23,

And he said, "What comes out of a person is what defiles him. For from within, out of the heart of man, come evil thoughts, sexual immorality, theft, murder, adultery, coveting, wickedness, deceit, sensuality, envy, slander, pride, foolishness. All these evil things come from within, and they defile a person.

Mark 10:11-12,

And he said to them, "Whoever divorces his wife and marries another commits adultery against her, and if she divorces her husband and marries another, she commits adultery.

Luke 16:18,

Everyone who divorces his wife and marries another commits adultery, and he who marries a woman divorced from her husband commits adultery.

Acts 15:20,

But should write to them to abstain from the things polluted by idols, and from sexual immorality, and from what has been strangled, and from blood.

Acts 15:20,

But should write to them to abstain from the things polluted by idols, and from sexual immorality, and from what has been strangled, and from blood.

Acts 15:29,

That you abstain from what has been sacrificed to idols, and from blood, and from what has been strangled, and from sexual immorality. If you keep yourselves from these, you will do well. Farewell.

Romans 1:24-27,

Therefore, God gave them up in the lusts of their hearts to impurity, to the dishonoring of their bodies among themselves, because they exchanged the truth about God for a lie and worshiped and served the creature rather than the Creator, who is blessed forever! Amen. For this reason, God gave them up to dishonorable passions. For their women exchanged natural relations for those that are contrary to nature; and the men likewise gave up natural relations with women and were consumed with passion for one another, men committing shameless acts with men and receiving in themselves the due penalty for their error.

Romans 8:12-13,

So then, brothers, we are debtors, not to the flesh, to live according to the flesh. For if you live according to the flesh you will die, but if by the Spirit you put to death the deeds of the body, you will live.

1 Corinthians 3:16-17,

Do you not know that you are God's temple and that God's Spirit dwells in you? If anyone destroys God's temple, God will destroy him. For God's temple is holy, and you are that temple.

1 Corinthians 5:1-5,

It is reported that there is sexual immorality among you, and of a kind that is not tolerated even among pagans, for a man has his father's wife. And you are arrogant! Ought you not rather to mourn? Let him who has done this be removed from among you. For though absent in body, I am present in spirit; and as if present, I have already pronounced judgment on the one who did such a thing. When you are assembled in the name of the Lord Jesus and my spirit is present, with the power of our Lord Jesus, you are to deliver this man to Satan for the destruction of the flesh, so that his spirit may be saved in the day of the Lord.

1 Corinthians 5:9-11,

I wrote to you in my letter not to associate with sexually immoral people— not at all meaning the sexually immoral of this world, or the greedy and swindlers, or idolaters, since then you would need to go out of the world. But now I am writing to you not to associate with anyone who bears the name of brother if he is guilty of sexual immorality or greed, or is an idolater, reviler, drunkard, or swindler—not even to eat with such a one.

1 Corinthians 6:9-11,

Or do you not know that the unrighteous will not inherit the kingdom of God? Do not be deceived: neither the sexually immoral, nor idolaters, nor adulterers, nor men who practice homosexuality, nor thieves, nor the greedy, nor drunkards, nor revilers, nor swindlers will inherit the kingdom of God. And such were some of you. But you were washed, you were sanctified, you were justified in the name of the Lord Jesus Christ and by the Spirit of our God.

1 Corinthians 6:13-20,

Food is meant for the stomach and the stomach for food"— and God will destroy both one and the other. The body is not meant for sexual immorality, but for the Lord, and the Lord for the body. And God raised the Lord and will also raise us up by his power. Do you not know that your bodies are members of Christ? Shall I then take the members of Christ and make them members of a prostitute? Never! Or do you not know that he who is joined to a prostitute becomes one body with her? For, as it is written, "The two will become one flesh." But he who is joined to the Lord becomes one spirit with him. Flee from sexual immorality. Every other sin a person commits is outside the body, but the sexually immoral person sins against his own body. Or do you not know that your body is a temple of the Holy Spirit within you, whom you have from God? You are not your own, for you were bought with a price. So glorify God in your body.

1 Corinthians 7:1-5,

Now concerning the matters about which you wrote: "It is good for a man not to have sexual relations with a woman." But because of the temptation to sexual immorality, each man should have his own wife and each woman her own husband. The husband should give to his wife her conjugal rights, and likewise the wife to her husband. For the wife does not have authority over her own body, but the husband does. Likewise, the husband does not have authority over his own body, but the wife does. Do not deprive one another, except perhaps by agreement for a limited time, that you may devote yourselves to prayer; but then come together again, so that Satan may not tempt you because of your lack of self-control.

1 Corinthians 10:8,

We must not indulge in sexual immorality as some of them did, and twenty-three thousand fell in a single day"

1 Corinthians 10:13,

No temptation has overtaken you that is not common to man. God is faithful, and he will not let you be tempted beyond your ability, but with the temptation he will also provide the way of escape, that you may be able to endure it.

2 Corinthians 12:21,

I fear that when I come again my God may humble me before you, and I may have to mourn over many of those who sinned earlier and have not repented of the impurity, sexual immorality, and sensuality that they have practiced.

Galatians 5 :16,

But I say, walk by the Spirit, and you will not gratify the desires of the flesh.

Galatians 5:19-21,

Now the works of the flesh are evident: sexual immorality, impurity, sensuality, idolatry, sorcery, enmity, strife, jealousy, fits of anger, rivalries, dissensions, divisions, envy, drunkenness, orgies, and things like these. I warn you, as I warned you before, that those who do such things will not inherit the kingdom of God.

Galatians 5:24,

And those who belong to Christ Jesus have crucified the flesh with its passions and desires.

Ephesians 4:19,

They have become callous and have given themselves up to sensuality, greedy to practice every kind of impurity.

Ephesians 5:3-5,

But sexual immorality and all impurity or covetousness must not even be named among you, as is proper among saints. Let there be no filthiness nor foolish talk nor crude joking, which are out of place, but instead let there be thanksgiving. For you may be sure of this, that everyone who is sexually immoral or impure, or who is covetous (that is, an idolater), has no inheritance in the kingdom of Christ and God.

Colossians 3:5,

Put to death therefore what is earthly in you: sexual immorality, impurity, passion, evil desire, and covetousness, which is idolatry.

1 Thessalonians 4:3-7,

For this is the will of God, your sanctification: that you abstain from sexual immorality; that each one of you know how to control his own body in holiness and honor, not in the passion of lust like the Gentiles who do not know God; that no one transgress and wrong his brother in this matter, because the Lord is an avenger in all these things, as we told you beforehand and solemnly warned you. For God has not called us for impurity, but in holiness.

1 Thessalonians 4:1-5,

Finally, then, brothers, we ask and urge you in the Lord Jesus, that as you received from us how you ought to walk and to please God, just as you are doing, that you do so more and more. For you know what instructions we gave you through the Lord Jesus. For this is the will of God, your sanctification: that you abstain from sexual immorality; that each one of you know how to control his own body in holiness and honor, not in the passion of lust like the Gentiles who do not know God.

Hebrews 12:16-17,

See that no one is sexually immoral, or unholy like Esau, who sold his birthright for a single meal. Afterward, as you know, when he wanted to inherit this blessing, he was rejected.

Hebrews 13:4,

Let marriage be held in honor among all, and let the marriage bed be undefiled, for God will judge the sexually immoral and adulterous.

James 1:12-15,

Blessed is the man who remains steadfast under trial, for when he has stood the test he will receive the crown of life, which God has promised to those who love him. Let no one say when he is tempted, "I am being tempted by God," for God cannot be tempted with evil, and he himself tempts no one. But each person is tempted when he is lured and enticed by his own desire. Then desire when it has conceived gives birth to sin, and sin when it is fully grown brings forth death.

1 Peter 2:11,

Beloved, I urge you as sojourners and exiles to abstain from the passions of the flesh, which wage war against your soul.

1 Peter 3:7,

Likewise, husbands, live with your wives in an understanding way, showing honor to the woman as the weaker vessel, since they are heirs with you of the grace of life, so that your prayers may not be hindered.

James 4:4,

You adulterous people! Do you not know that friendship with the world is enmity with God? Therefore, whoever wishes to be a friend of the world makes himself an enemy of God.

1 John 2:3-4,

And by this we know that we have come to know him, if we keep his commandments. Whoever says "I know him" but does not keep his commandments is a liar, and the truth is not in him.

1 John 2:16,

For all that is in the world—the desires of the flesh and the desires of the eyes and pride in possessions—is not from the Father, but is from the world.

Jude 1:4,

For certain people have crept in unnoticed who long ago were designated for this condemnation, ungodly people, who pervert the grace of our God into sensuality and deny our only Master and Lord, Jesus Christ.

Jude 1:7,

Just as Sodom and Gomorrah and the surrounding cities, which likewise indulged in sexual immorality and pursued unnatural desire, serve as an example by undergoing a punishment of eternal fire.

Revelation 2:14, 16a,

Jesus speaking: Nevertheless, I have a few things against you: You have people there who hold to the teaching of Balaam, who taught Balak to entice the Israelites to sin by eating food sacrificed to idols and by committing sexual immorality…Repent therefore!

Revelation 2:20-23,

Jesus speaking: Nevertheless, I have this against you: You tolerate that woman Jezebel, who calls herself a prophetess. By her teaching she misleads my servants into sexual immorality and the eating of food sacrificed to idols. I have given her time to repent of her immorality, but she is unwilling. So I will cast her on a bed of suffering, and I will make those who commit adultery with her suffer intensely, unless they repent of her ways. I will strike her children dead. Then all the churches will know that I am He who searches hearts and minds, and I will repay each of you according to your deeds.

Revelation 21:8,

But as for the cowardly, the faithless, the detestable, as for murderers, the sexually immoral, sorcerers, idolaters, and all liars, their portion will be in the lake that burns with fire and sulfur, which is the second death.

Revelation 22: 14-15,

Jesus speaking: "Blessed are those who wash their robes, that they may have the right to the tree of life and may go through the gates into the city. Outside are the dogs, those who practice magic arts, the sexually immoral, the murders, then idolaters and everyone who loves and practices falsehood.

Revelation 22:19,

And if anyone takes words away from this book of prophecy, God will take away from him his share in the tree of life and in the holy city, which are described in this book.

WHERE AND HOW JESUS' APOSTLES DIED

James, the son of Zebedee, who was executed by Herod about AD 44 (Acts 12:2). Read how each of the apostles spread out to minister and evangelize, and how many of the apostles died for their faith.

Peter and Paul
Both were martyred in Rome about AD 66, during the persecution under Emperor Nero. Paul was beheaded. Peter was crucified upside down at his request since he did not feel worthy to die in the same manner as his Lord.

Andrew
He went to the "land of the man-eaters" in what is now the Soviet Union. Christians there claim him as the first to bring the gospel to their land. He also preached in Asia Minor, modern-day Turkey, and Greece, where **he is said to have been crucified**.

Thomas
He was probably most active in the area east of Syria. Tradition has him preaching as far east as India, where the ancient Marthoma Christians revere him as their founder. They claim that he died there when **pierced through with the spears** of four soldiers.

Philip
He possibly had a powerful ministry in Carthage in North Africa and Asia Minor, where he converted the wife of a Roman proconsul. In retaliation, the proconsul had Philip arrested and **cruelly put to death**.

Matthew

He was the tax collector, and writer of a Gospel ministered in Persia and Ethiopia. Some of the oldest reports say he was not martyred, while others say he was **stabbed to death** in Ethiopia.

Bartholomew

He had widespread missionary travels attributed to him by tradition: to India with Thomas and back to Armenia, Ethiopia, and Southern Arabia. There are various accounts of how **he met his death as a martyr** for the gospel.

James

He was **the son of Alpheus** and is one of at least three James referred to in the New Testament. There is some confusion as to which is which, but this James is reckoned to have ministered in Syria. The Jewish historian Josephus reported that he was **stoned and then clubbed to death.**

Simon, the Zealot

As the story goes, he ministered in Persia and was **killed** after refusing to sacrifice to the sun god.

Matthias

He was the apostle chosen to replace Judas. Tradition sends him to Syria **with Andrew and to death by burning.**

John

The only one of the apostles generally thought to have died a natural death from old age. He was the church leader in the Ephesus area and is said to have taken care of Mary the mother of Jesus in his home. During Domitian's persecution in the middle '90s, he was exiled to the island of Patmos. There he is credited with writing the last book of the New Testament—Revelation.

Note: Info: Source: Christianity Today.

This particular note refers to the above-mentioned information concerning Jesus' apostles

APPENDIX C
SIGNIFICANCE OF THE REDEFINITION OF MARRIAGE

(Hank Unplugged Short)
Bible Answer Man
Jan 9, 2023

Hank Hanegraaff, president of the Christian Research Institute and host of the Bible Answer Man broadcast, explains why the redefinition of marriage is such a serious matter. In the considered opinions of such great western philosophers as Socrates, Plato, and Aristotle, marriage was seen as a relationship between men and women. Indeed, in the Judeo-Christian tradition marriage has always been rooted in the dual, gender-distinct nature of humanity. As such, intercourse consummates marriage as a multifaceted mystery in which two people are forged together as one flesh. In mysterious union, a man and a woman procreate children fashioned in the image and likeness of their Creator.

Marriage, however, is even more profound than procreation and paradisiacal pleasure—it **is a mysterious parable of Christ and His church**. The union of two people a poignant portrait of **the unity of Christ and His bride**. The parable has its roots in Genesis and bears ultimate fruit in Revelation. There are essentially three building blocks of civil society—marriage, church, government—resting atop the foundation of human life. Of the three none is more significant than marriage. The ABC'S—Anthropology: women and men enjoy strategic complementarity; as such, both are essential in the rearing of children. Biology: sexual reproduction requires male and female. Civics: Redefining marriage opens Pandora's Box and spells the death knell to civil society.

A GENTLEMAN'S RULES FOR CULTIVATING MORAL VALUES IN THE HOME

From an 1880s Manual on Manners
The Epoch Times, March 19, 2023

Home Culture

The work of home culture should be made a matter of great importance to everyone, for upon it depends on the happiness of earthly homes, as well as our fitness for the enjoyment of the eternal home in heaven. The sufferings endured here, friend for friend, parents for children, unrequited sacrifices, cares and tears, all tend to discipline us, and prepare us for the recompense which eternity brings.

Cultivate Moral Courage

Moral courage will be cultivated in your children as they observe that you say and do whatever you conscientiously believe to be right and true, without being influenced by the views of others; thus, showing them that you fear nothing so much as failing to do your duty. Perhaps this may be difficult to do, but every mother can at least show her appreciation of moral courage when she sees it exhibited by others, and in this way incite its growth in the souls of her children. Moral courage is a rare endowment, and those who possess it can act with perfect independence of the opinions of others, and govern themselves only by the laws of propriety, uprightness and charity.

The Pernicious Influence of Indolence

If you would preserve your children from the pernicious influence of indolence and all its corrupting tendencies, you must be earnest in purpose, active, energetic and fervent in spirit. Earnestness sharpens the faculties; indolence corrodes and dulls them. By the former we rise higher and higher, by the latter we sink lower and lower. Indolence begets discontent, envy and jealousy, while labor elevates the mind and character. Cultivate in your children's habits of thought which will keep their minds occupied upon something that will be of use or advantage, and prevent them from acquiring habits of idleness, if you would secure their future well-being.

It has been said that he who performs no useful act in society, who makes no human being happier, is leading a life of utter selfishness—a life of sin—for a life of selfishness is a life of sin. There is nowhere room for idleness. Work is both a duty and a necessity of our nature, and a befitting reward will ever follow it. To foster and encourage labor in some useful form, is a duty which parents should urge upon their children, if they should seek their best good.

Self-Respect

It is the mother's duty to see that her children protect themselves from the many pitfalls which surround them, such as malice, envy, conceit, avariciousness, and other evils, by being clad in the armor of self-respect; and then they will be able to encounter temptation and corruption, unstained and unpolluted. This feeling of self-respect is something stronger than self-reliance, higher than pride. It is an energy of the soul which master's the whole being for its good, watching with a never-ceasing vigilance. It is the sense of duty, and the sense of honor combined. It is an armor, which, though powerless to shield from sorrows that purify and invigorate, yet will avert all hostile influences that assail, from whatever source they come. The mother having once made her children conscious that always and everywhere they carry with them such an angel to shield, warn and rescue them, may let them go out into the world, and fear nothing from the wiles and temptations which may beset them.

Result of Good Breeding in the Home Circle

The laws of good breeding in no place bear more gratifying results than in the home circle. Here, tempered with love, and nurtured by all kindly impulses, they bear the choicest fruit. A true lady will show as much courtesy, and observe the duties of politeness as unfailingly, toward every member of her family as toward her most distinguished guest. A true gentleman will feel bound to exercise courtesy and kindness in his intercourse with those who depend upon him for protection and example. Children influenced by such examples at home, will never fail to show to their elders the respect due them, to their young companions the same consideration for their feelings which they expect to meet with in return, nor to servants that patience which even the best too often require. In such a home peace and good will are the household gods.

Fault-Finding and Grumbling

The oil of civility is required to make the wheels of domestic life run smoothly. The habit of fault-finding and grumbling indulged in by some, is an exceedingly vexatious one, and will, in time, ruffle the calmest spirit and the sweetest temper. It is the little annoyances, perplexities and misfortunes which often render life a burden; the little omission of minor duties and the committing of little faults that perpetually scourge us and keep the heart sore. Constant fault-finding, persistent misrepresentations of motives, suspicions of evil where no evil was intended, will complete the work in all but the finest and most heroic natures. They alone can stand the fiery test, coming out purer and stronger for the ordeal. Children who habitually obey the commandment, "Be kind to one another," will find in mature life, how strong the bonds of affection may be that bind the members of the household together.

Family Jars Not to be made Public

Whatever may be the family disagreements, they should never be made known outside of the home circle, if it can be avoided. Those who expose the faults of the members of their family are severely judged by the world, and no provocation can be a good excuse for it. It is exceedingly vulgar, not to say un-Christian, for members of the same family, to be at enmity with one another.

Yielding To One Another

One of the greatest disciplines of human life, is that which teaches us to yield our wills to those who have a claim upon us to do so, even in trifling, every-day affairs; the wife to the husband, children to parents, to teachers and to one another. In cases where principle is concerned, it is, of course, necessary to be firm, which requires an exercise of moral courage.

Conflicting Interests

Conflicting interests are a fruitful source of family difficulties. The command of Christ to the two brothers who came to Him with their disputes, "Beware of covetousness," is as applicable among members of the same family now, as it was when those words were spoken. It is better that you have few or no business transactions with anyone who is near and dear to you and connected by family ties. In business relations men are apt to be very exact, because of their habits of business, and this exactness is too often construed by near friends and relatives as actuated by purely selfish motives. Upon this rock many a bark of family love has been wrecked.

Religious Education

It is well to remember that every blessing of our lives, every joy of our hearts and every ray of hope shed upon our pathway, have had their origin in religion, and may be traced in all their hallowed, healthful influences on the Bible. With the dawn of childhood, then, in the earliest days of intelligence, should the mind be impressed and stored with religious truth, and nothing should be allowed to exclude or efface it. It should be taught so early that the mind will never remember when it began to learn; it will then have the character of innate, inbred principles, incorporated with their very being.

Obedience

If you would not have all your instructions and counsels ineffectual, teach your children to obey. Government in a family is the great safeguard of religion and morals, the support of order and the source of prosperity. Nothing has a greater tendency to bring a curse upon a family than the insubordination and disobedience of children, and there is no more painful and disgusting sight than an ungoverned child.

Influence of Example

Never forget that the first book children read is their parents' example— their daily deportment. If this is forgotten you may find, in the loss of your domestic peace, that while your children well know the right path, they follow the wrong. Childhood is like a mirror, catching and reflecting images all around it. Remember that an impious, profane or vulgar thought may operate upon the heart of a young child like a careless spray of water upon polished steel, staining it with rust that no efforts can thoroughly efface. Improve the first ten years of life as the golden opportunity, which may never return. It is the seed time, and your harvest depends upon the seed then sown.

The Influence of Books

Few mothers can over-estimate the influence which the companionship of books exerts in youth upon the habits and tastes of their children, and no mother who has the welfare of her children at heart will neglect the important work of choosing the proper books for them to read, while they are under her care. She should select for them such as will both interest and instruct, and this should be done during the early years, before their minds shall have imbibed the pernicious teachings of bad books and sensational novels. The poison imbibed from bad books works so secretly that their influence for evil is even greater than the influence of bad associates.

The mother has it in her power to make such books the companions and friends of her children as her good judgment may select, and to impress upon them their truths, by conversing with them about the moral lessons or the intellectual instructions they contain. A taste may be easily cultivated for books on natural science and for history, as well as for those that teach important and wholesome lessons for the young, such as are contained in the works of Mrs. Edgeworth, Mrs. Child, Mrs. Yonge, and many other books written for the young.

The above is an excerpt from "Our Deportment," a code of manners, conduct, and dress of refined society by John H. Young A.M., published in 1881. We offer it in hopes of promoting gentlemanly conduct among men— young and older—in today's sometimes unbalanced and undisciplined world.

GOD's PRESENT CREATION and FUTURE RECREATION INITIATIVE REVEALED ONLY IN THE BIBLE

The biblical description of the beginning of God's present creation of the heavens and earth is described in Genesis 1. The highlight in that initial divine creation is the creation of the first two people: Adam and Eve, in Genesis 2. It is this creation action that may seem to us, human beings, of greatest interest, as it tells us that there are only two kinds of human beings: men and women. Procreation of human beings comes only through a relationship between a man and a woman. This is a fundamental creation standard for the ongoing creation of only two kinds of people: boys and girls growing into mature men and women.

This primary foundation of the furtherance of mankind throughout the centuries has been, in a very early stage, injured by the so-called 'Fall of Man' described in Genesis 3. In the Bible book: Ezekiel, chapters 1-3, we hear also about angels and how God uses them in relationship with human beings.

We learn that there are God-obeying angels as there are disobedient angels who are listening to the fallen arch angel Satan, also called Lucifer. It is in Genesis 3 that we read about Satan approaching both Adam and Eve, and how he succeeded in having both Adam and Eve becoming disobedient to God. As a result, all descendants of the two sinful people, Adam and Eve, all mankind were borne with a sinful nature and in principle lived as sinful people in disobedience to God.

Both the Bible's Old Testament and the New Testament describe God working with sinful people helping them, with the help of the Holy Spirit, to live up to God's principles of living through a loving relationship with Jesus Christ. In the Old Testament we read about the unfolding story of God working with His specially chosen people, called Jews. As God's original covenant people, the Jews, though most often living in disobedience to God, had to deal with the consequence of their immoral lifestyles.

ABOUT THE AUTHOR

For twenty years, working as a Mechanical Design Engineer and Industrial Engineer (Management Operation) in the Netherlands and later on in Calgary, Canada, following emigration in 1973. In 1979, transitioning from industry to ministry, beginning with 3 years of Seminary education (M.Div.) following 1 year at a local Christian college/presently university, both located in Grand Rapids, MI, to make the transition from engineer to being a pastor. During the next twenty-one years, serving as a pastor in Alberta and British Columbia, while taking continuing education. Receiving a Master's degree (Th.M.) in Domestic Missiology (1998) and a Doctoral degree (D. Min.) in Ecclesiology. Certified Short-Term Counselor (2001). As pastor emeritus, traveling for nine years (2007-2015) to Uganda, three months per year for teaching at Uganda Christian University (UCU) in Mukono during the first two years. Then, seven more years teaching at All Saints University, Lango (ASUL) in Lira, Northern Uganda, including preaching and making field trips to villages on behalf of several churches. Those villages received financial support from various churches in Calgary for economic development projects. Since then, writing four books in seven to eight years, including this present book.

Also, from this Author

The first two books of the so-called OKELLO TRILOGY, prior to the third and present book, "*The Royal Deal: Making the Case for the One Everlasting Church*" are:

BOOK ONE: "*THE REAL DEAL: Making the Case for the One True God,*" 2018. On Amazon.

This book explains differences between the contents of the Bible and the Qur'an, between the God of the Bible and Allah of the Quran. Such comparison leads to the real identity of Allah with his hate for especially Jews and Christians. Many examples of explicit Muslim's inhuman behavior substantiate the global radical-Muslim threat to destroy Jewish and Christian communities throughout the world. This book helps readers understand that there is a significant and most strenuous spiritual battle going on. This spiritual battle is reflected in the hearts and minds of men and women today. This book also suggests how Christians need to be united in a biblical response to the growing threat of militant Islam to bring the entire world under the rule of Sharia law and worship of Islam's Allah.

BOOK TWO: "*THE RIGHT DEAL: Making the Case for a More Respectful Society*, 2020. On Amazon.

This book explains the alarming and developing influence from radical-liberal ideology on political, social and spiritual

matters in the US and Canada. In Canada, various political parties oppose long-existing Judeo-Christian values, norms and principles. In the US, the Far Left shows similar disrespect for the same long-held values, norms and principles. The history of radical liberalism reveals the immense human suffering it has already caused in the world. We may expect that today's radical liberals, in Canada and the US, are leading our long-enjoyed freedoms and democracy along a slippery slope towards a new socio-political situation, in which there are no moral absolutes. This book seeks ways to protect and to show respect for all human beings. This book hopes to reach more and more Christians who need to "wake up" to the reality of today's anti-Christ revolution.

BOOK THREE: "*THE ROYAL DEAL: Making the Case for the One Everlasting Church*. Hopefully, this book will be published on Amazon early 2025.

Note: With this third book, the "3. R. DEAL" TRILOGY is finished. A more informal title of this trilogy is the "OKELLO"[63] Trilogy.

[63] OKELLO is an African name given to me during my 3-months periods during 9 consecutive years at a Christian university in Northern Uganda. The name OKELLO means 'He who brings fortune."

In adding, I wish to comment that reading the meaning of the name OKELLO one would agree that this name perfectly suits our Lord Jesus Christ!

Apart from this trilogy another book has been written, entitled,

"THE RAINBOW LETTERS: Immorality: The Church's Achilles Heel" (May 2022). Author: Rev. Peter Hendriks Okello.

ACKNOWLEDGEMENTS

As my previous book, "THE RIGHT DEAL" was introduced as "The Okello Sequel" thereby including my first book, entitled "THE REAL DEAL." With this present book, "THE ROYAL DEAL" we finish the final **"3. R. DEAL"** trilogy. All three books are meant to help the reader understand that, and how Christian men and women, are experiencing serious resistance from especially radical Muslims and radical Liberals since the last number of years and continues.

As has been the case with the preparation of the previous two books of the presently so called **"3. R. DEAL"** trilogy**,** my wife Louisa deserves much thankfulness for her love, patience and support during the many years of writing this trilogy and another book on especially Immorality. The almost seven years of time spent on writing those books is one thing, but the time to think about what and how to write them down in a concise manner is a different matter all together.

The above words lead me to thank God and thus including specifically the involvement of the Holy Spirit by providing me the much-needed time, energy and the development of thoughts and the writing of so many hours to develop these four books during the last seven years. It is the presence, encouragement and guidance of the Holy Spirit that I have been able to discern the times we live in and will continue to be in for years to come, and to prepare the trilogy plus one extra book.

Then I want to thank my Christian friend, Rudy Muller, for his time to pre-read my book and to draw my attention to what needs to be done to improve the text.